TRAINING
AND DEVELOPMENT

TRAINING AND DEVELOPMENT

AN ESSENTIAL GUIDE FOR STUDENTS & PRACTITIONERS;
INCLUDES 30+ READY TO USE TEMPLATES

DR. YOGESH PAHUJA

PARTRIDGE
A Penguin Random House Company

Copyright © 2015 by Dr. Yogesh Pahuja.

ISBN: Softcover   978-1-4828-4884-7
       eBook   978-1-4828-4883-0

All rights reserved. No part of this book may be used or reproduced by any means, graphic, electronic, or mechanical, including photocopying, recording, taping or by any information storage retrieval system without the written permission of the publisher except in the case of brief quotations embodied in critical articles and reviews.

Because of the dynamic nature of the Internet, any web addresses or links contained in this book may have changed since publication and may no longer be valid. The views expressed in this work are solely those of the author and do not necessarily reflect the views of the publisher, and the publisher hereby disclaims any responsibility for them.

Print information available on the last page.

To order additional copies of this book, contact
Partridge India
000 800 10062 62
orders.india@partridgepublishing.com

www.partridgepublishing.com/india

CONTENTS

Preface ix
Acknowledgements xi

Part- 1: The Training Cycle & OD concept.

1. Organizational Development 1
   - Introduction of OD 3
   - Definitions of OD 4
   - Growth & Relevance of OD 6
   - Four Pillars of OD 8
   - Organizational Development Practitioner 11
   - Future of OD: A Thought 14
2. An Introduction To Training 15
   - Introduction 17
   - Training versus Formal education 19
   - Role of Trainer 20
   - Training Cycle 21
   - Adult Learning Styles 22
   - How do Adults learn? 24
3. Strategic Perspective Of Training 27
   - Strategic Perspective of Training 29
4. Training Need Analysis 31
   - Introduction 33
   - Identification of Training Needs 35
   - What is a training need? 36
   - Process for training needs identification 37
   - Training Need Identification Methods 38
   - Three Levels of Training Need Identification 38
   - The nine step Training Needs analysis process 42
   - Needs Analysis Model 43
5. Training Design 45
   - Training Objective 47

- Training content & Delivery 48
- Designing methods 51
- Training methods that work 53

6 Training Evaluation 65
- Measuring effectiveness of training 67
- Training Evaluation: Result Based Approach 68
- Level based models of Training Evaluation 70
- Understanding levels of Training Evaluation 72
- Appropriate Post-program Data Collection Methods 78

Part- 2: Evaluate Training and Development

1 Concept, Definition and Need for Evaluation 81
- Introduction 83
- Concept 83
- Definition 84

2 Role of Evaluator 85
- Role of Evaluator 87

3 Stages of Evaluation 89
- Introduction 91
- Typologies of Evaluation 93

4 Evaluation Methods 97
- Introduction 99
- Pre-training evaluation 99
- Evaluation during training 102
- Post Training Evaluation: 104
- Job Behaviour Evaluation 108
- Job Improvement Plan: 112
- Ultimate Value Evaluation: 112
- Follow-Up results: 112

5 Criteria & approaches for
  Selection of Evaluation Methods 115
- Introduction 117
- Ultimate Value Approach: 117

- Trainee Centered Approach: 118
- Training Centered Approach: 119

6 Techniques of Measurement and Its related Problems 121
- Introduction 123
- Quantitative Approaches of Measuring: 123
- Rating Scales: 131

Part- 3: Ready to use Templates

- Training Proposal Template 1: 139
- Training Proposal Template 2 140
- Training Proposal Template 3 141
- Training Need Identification Template 1 142
- Training Need Identification/ Assessment Template 2 147
- Training Need Identification/ Assessment Template 3 149
- Training Need Identification Template 4 152
- Training Need Identification Template 5 154
- Training Need Identification Template 6 156
- Training Need Identification Template 7 158
- Training Registration Form Template 1 160
- Training Registration Form Template 2 162
- Training Registration Form Template 3: 164
- Training Design Template 1 166
- Training Design Template 2 167
- Training Design Template 3 168
- Training Design Template 4 170
- Training Calendar Template 1 171
- Training Calendar Template 2 171
- Training Calendar Template 3 172
- Training Calendar Template 4 173
- Training Evaluation Template 1 174
- Training Evaluation Template 2 176
- Training Evaluation Template 3 177
- Training Evaluation Template 4 178

- Training Evaluation Template 5 181
- Training Evaluation Template 6 182
- Training Evaluation Template 7 183
- Training Certificate Template 1 184
- Training Certificate Template 2 185
- Training Certificate Template 3 185
- Training Certificate Template 4 186

Notes/References 187

PREFACE

The need for this book arose at the time when a leading B School in the country approached me to design and deliver a course on Training and Development. I took up the assignment and understood the contents to be covered. After searching several sources for the content, I realized that there isn't a single book-source, which gives applicable knowledge of T&D in a capsule. Thus I started to work on the subject to include most relevant topics and limit the need to refer several sources.

I realized that T&D applications are best understood with a basic foundation in OD as a functional area and its application in the industry. Thus the book begins with an over view on understanding OD and then takes on the complete training cycle in a sequence. Part I of the book therefore covers the conceptual understanding of OD and T&D as a subject.

I have noticed in the past 20 years of my work experience as a trainer that most organizations refer only to Kirkpatrick model of training evaluation and several practitioners are not even aware of other models that exist for training evaluation. In fact I received a request to prepare and build content on training evaluation additionally to enable the students and practitioners to apply it at work place suitably. Thus part II of the book cover the much needed 'know-how' on training evaluation.

A book on training and development would be incomplete if it did not offer sample of formats to be used for preparing a training proposal, training calendar or how to identify training needs. Thus part III of the book is a compilation of over 30 such forms which are ready to use and can be modified suitably to an organizations requirement.

Why attempt to reinvent the wheel when you can have all the raw material and spares to design one of your own suitable to your need. This is exactly the purpose of this book, i.e. as a ready reckoner for students and practitioners to apply it professionally at work.

Your feedback and comments are welcome. Feel free to write to me at yogesh.pahuja@hotmail.com

ACKNOWLEDGEMENTS

The first heartfelt thank you goes to the B school and its faculty for initiating me to develop content on training and development. Also to the all my clients who permitted me to serve them by offering my services as a trainer and building upon my knowledge through learning by experience.

I have learnt a lot from all of my students and workshop delegates who have attended my sessions and motivated me to give my best.

In the process of development of this book as a final version, it would be incomplete if I did not acknowledge the efforts of my student and now my professional colleague Gaurang Patel who spent hours on it for editing and Surabhi Poduval for proof reading.

I dedicate this book to my Parents Dr. O.P.Pahuja and Mrs. P.L.Pahuja with whose support and direction I have reached here today. Their encouragement and support in my academic and professional ventures is priceless.

Further I would also like to acknowledge my PhD Guide Dr. D.M.Pestonjee (retd. Prof. of IIM Ahmedabad) who is a true source of inspiration and a role model for all my academic pursuits. The contributions and learning from Dr. S.M.Khan who also helped me during my doctorate, deserves a special mention here.

And last but not the least, I would like to thank my lovely wife Nilam, for being a true support and believing in me.

PART- I
The Training Cycle & OD concept.

CHAPTER 1

Organizational Development

Introduction of OD

Can you think for a moment about the organizations to which you belong? You probably have many to name, such as your company, a school, volunteer organization, or a political party. You are undoubtedly influenced by many other organizations in your life, such as a health care organization like a doctor's office or hospital, a temple group, a child's school, a bank, or the local city council or state government.

You can take name of the organization/s with which you are not happy. It might be the one, which you left behind because you did not have the opportunity to contribute that you would have liked. Maybe it was a dissatisfying team atmosphere, or you were not appreciated or recognized for the time and energy that you dedicated to the job.

You've likely had some excellent experiences in organizations, too. You may have had a job that was especially fulfilling or where you learned a great deal and coworkers became good friends. Maybe your local volunteer organization helped a number of people through organized fundraisers or other social services activities.

Perhaps you joined or started a local community group to successfully campaign against the decision of your local city council or school board. All of this is to demonstrate what you already know intuitively, that we spend a great deal of our lives working in, connected to, and affected by organizations. Some of these organizations function quite well, whereas others struggle. Some are quite rewarding environments in which to work or participate, but in others, organizational members are frustrated, neglected, and disengaged. With the help of OD we can make organization more effective and productive and at the same time more rewarding, satisfying, and engaging places in which to work and participate. By learning about the field of organization development and the process by which it is conducted, you will be a more effective change agent inside the organizations to which you belong.

Organizational Development (OD) is any process intending to increase individual & organizational effectiveness by applying principles of Behavioral science.

The chief idea is to target the human resources, teach & train them & make them better performers, thus enhancing the effectiveness of the entire organization. This is an attempt to make organizations more hospitable to Employees.

In this age of fast paced Internet companies & emerging knowledge based global economy; the leaders are the ones who create changes.

Definitions of OD

The practice of OD covers a wide spectrum of activities with even more number of variations in them. Team building, structural change in organizations, job enrichment, etc are most common of them. OD also addresses change management.

Number of definitions exists for Organizational Development. Each definition has a slightly different emphasis.

The most optimum definition derived out of the all the above definitions is

"Organizational Development is a system wide application of behavioral science knowledge to planned development, improvement, & reinforcement of the strategies, structures & processes that lead to organizational effectiveness" –Cummings & Worley

This definition differentiates OD from other approaches to organizational change like management consulting, technological innovations, operations management, & training & development.

First, OD applies to strategy, structure & processes covering the entire system, such as an organization, a single plant or a department. A change program aimed at modifying an organization's strategy for example might focus on how the organization relates to a wider environment & on how those relationships can be improved. Another program could be devised to help top management to become more effective by focusing on interactions & problem-solving processes within the groups. Activities like training & development, technological innovations, reengineering might focus on a single or fewer aspects of the system. The attention in these activities is narrowed to individuals within the system.

Secondly, OD is based on behavioral science knowledge & practice, including micro concepts like leadership, group dynamics, work design, & macro concepts like strategy, organizational design, relations etc.

OD is more of an adaptive process for planning & implementing change than a blueprint for how things should be done. The plans are flexible & can be changed as new information is gathered. OD involves both creation & subsequent reinforcement of the change. For example, implementing self-managed work teams might focus on giving more freedom to workers. After workers have more control, attention would shift to check that supervisors continue to provide freedom.

Finally, OD is oriented to improve organizational effectiveness. This involves 2 major assumptions. First, an effective organization is able to solve its own problems & focus its attention on using its resources to achieve its goals. Organizational development helps organizational members to gain the skills & knowledge necessary to conduct these activities by involving them in the process. Second, an effective organization has high performance, including financial returns, quality products & services, high productivity, continuous improvement & a high quality of work life. The organization's performance responds well to the expectations of the external stakeholders like the customers, suppliers, distributors, government agencies & others who provide the organization with the supplies & legitimacy.

OD differs with change management & organizational change. Both OD & change management addresses the effective implementation of planned change. They are concerned with the sequence of activities, processes & leadership issues that produce organizational improvement. They differ in the underlying Value Orientation. OD's behavioral science foundation supports values of human potential, participation, & development whereas change management is more focused on values of economic potential & creation of competitive advantage.

Organization change is a broader concept than OD. It is concerned with any kind of change, including technical, managerial innovations, organizational decline, or the evolution of a system over time. These changes may or may not be directed at making the organization more developed like OD.

Growth & Relevance of OD

In this age of globalization OD could help the organizations to create effective responses to organizational changes & in many cases even proactively influence the strategic directions of the firm.

If we look carefully, the changes could be classified into three major ones.

The first of the trend is globalization. The markets in this era are changing. New markets are being explored; new governments & changes in the Politics have opened many new avenues for the Producers. The issues of erstwhile era like the unionization of workers, strikes are loosing their presences. Communities like ASEAN, European Union & others have started joining hands to co-operate in matters of trade. Economies like China have created open market Economies.

Secondly, IT is redefining the traditional business model by changing how the work is performed, how the knowledge is used, & how the cost of doing the business is calculated. Organizations are sourcing the latest technology to lower the costs of operations. Technology is used to collect, store, manipulate, transmit in a more systematic & meaningful manner, with added benefit –At Lower cost. The rate of innovations is so high that it hardly takes a couple of years for a technology to become obsolete. The universe of information available from the internet& the easier ways to share information has given birth to a new form of work culture called Telecommuting.

Information technology is also changing the way knowledge is used. Organization members share the key information that was once only under the control of the senior management.

Third wave of change is managerial innovation. This has made a very profound impact on the way of doing tasks. Innovations have taken cues from IT & Globalization to create newer trends & more effective business models. New organizational forms like networks, strategic alliances, & virtual corporations provide organizations with inputs to enhance production, & delivery. Strategic alliances have emerged as one of the indispensable tools to excel. Methods of change such as Destaffing

& reengineering have radically reduced the size of the organizations & increased the flexibility.

The tools like search conferences & open space have increased the speed at which the organizational change takes place.

OD Practitioners argue that these forces are not only powerful in their own but also interrelated. Their interaction makes the environment highly uncertain. Hence organizations are becoming dependent on interventions, changes and restructuring to survive & prosper. They are up to making the processes more streamlined & nimble & more responsive to external demands. OD is playing an increasingly key role in helping organizations change themselves. It is helping organizations assess themselves & their environments, & revitalize & rebuild their strategies, structures & processes.

The changes made are not just superficial but transform the underlying assumptions & values governing their behaviors. OD professionals find respected positions as internal consultants serving a particular organization or even as an external consultant practicing independently.

A career in OD could be really rewarding providing challenges & interesting assignments while working with managers & employees to improve their organizations & their work lives.

But beyond that, OD finds a role in the profile of each & every managers & CEO's. All of them are responsible for supervising & developing subordinates, & improving their departments. The work force also needs to be aware of the newer technologies & trends.

Overall OD can help managers & personnel by providing the necessary skills & knowledge for establishing effective interpersonal & helping relationships. In a nutshell the field is of high relevance in today's era.

Four Pillars of OD

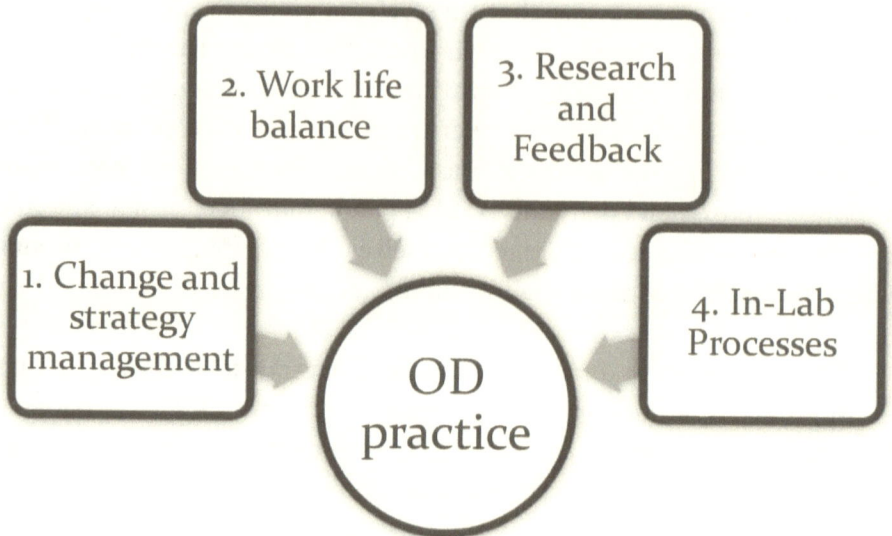

The current day OD has evolved from the above mentioned 4 Pillars. The description about these Pillars would throw some light on the history of OD.

1. **Change and strategy management:**

Change and strategies management has become an integral part of OD. This is a recent development in field of OD that focuses on Organizational vision, mission and also takes into account strategic goals of business.

As organizations and their technological, political and social environments have become more complex & more uncertain, the scale & intricacies of organizational change have increased. This trend has produced the need for a strategic perspective from OD & encouraged planned change processes at the organizational level.

Change and strategy management involves improving the alignment among an organization's environment, strategy, & organizational design. Change interventions include efforts to improve both organizations' relationship to its environment & the fit between its technical, political & cultural systems.

2. Work Life Balance (WLB):

The focus on Work life Balance and integrating technology with people was first started in Europe in the early 1960's. This involved joint participation by unions & management in design of work & led to work design that gave the employees, high level of discretion, task variety, & feedback about results.

This also led to existence of self-managed teams as a concept got initiated which composed of multi level of workers and gave them enough autonomy to manage their own performances.

People started to define WLB in terms of specific techniques & approaches used for improving work. It was viewed as synonymous with Job enrichment; self managed teams, & labor management committees.

WLB as a concept spread to other countries as organizations focused on providing quality at a low price. The Japanese undoubtedly managed to have an advantage and expanded their focus into other areas of work place that could affect employee productivity, satisfaction regard to physical work environment. They even introduced concepts like Quality circles.

3. Research & Feedback:

Research and feedback became a true pillar for organizational development as every component needed data collection, analysis of data, its reporting and application. Even a small component of how a person felt or what his attitude was, needed to be recorded in not only quality but quantity; such that statistical treatment to the collected data provides useful inferences.

The purpose of this research was primarily to use the data for their own problems and also to initiate change within the organization.

Among the pioneering action research studies was the work of Lewin & his students at Harwood manufacturing company & the classic research by Lester Coch & John French on overcoming a resistance to change. The later studies led to participative management as means of getting employees involved in planning & managing change.

A key component of most action studies was the systematic collection of survey data that was fed back to the client organization.

Other research in this arena included Renesis Likert's dissertation on "A Technique for measurement of attitudes". He used a five point scale that came to be known as Likert scale.

The feedback process that evolved was an interlocking chain of conferences. The major findings was first reported to the top management & then transmitted to the entire organization. Feedback sessions were conducted in task groups & the process led to discussion among supervisors & subordinates. The pattern of data collection, data feedback, action planning, implementation & follow –up data collection in both action research & Survey feedback is common.

4. In-Lab processes:

The first In-Lab process was initiated by growth of the National Training Laboratories (NTL) & development of training groups or sensitivity training or T-groups/L-groups training. The T-group is a small, unstructured group in which participants learn from their own interactions & evolving dynamics about the issues such as interpersonal relationships & personal growth, leadership & group dynamics. For an In-Lab process, a workshop was conducted where the community leaders were called up & they discussed the problems. At the end of each day, the researchers privately discussed the group behavior & dynamics they had observed. The community leaders were willing to have a feedback on the session. Thus this was the first T-group, in which people reacted about the data on their own behavior.

The researchers primarily drew conclusions that the process of group building has a potential for learning that can be transferred to other situations.

Organizational Development Practitioner

OD professional have traditionally shared a common set of humanistic values promoting open communications, employee involvement, & personal development. They deeply study the social processes in organization. In the contemporary era, OD professionals have expanded those traditional values & skills to include more concern on organizational effectiveness, competitiveness, & bottom-line results & a greater attention to technical, structural & strategic parts of organization. They may be internal or external consultants who offer services to client organizations.

They specialize in variety of areas like reward system, organizational design, total quality, information technology, & business strategy. These fields are becoming integrated with Process orientation.

Even Line managers have become OD practitioners in a very true sense. They apply the principles of OD in their own area of Specialization or expertise in order to achieve better results.

The table below depicts the Knowledge & Skills required by An OD Practitioner:

Knowledge based skills

FOUNDATION skills	CORE skills
1. **Organizational Behavior** • Work Culture • Work Design • Interpersonal relations • Power & Politics • Leadership • Goal Setting • Conflict • Ethics 2. **Group Dynamics** • Roles • Communication Processes • Decision Making Processes • Stages of Group Development • Leadership 3. **Management & Organizational Theory** • Planning, Organizing, leading & controlling • Problem Solving & decision making • Systems theory • Contingency theory • Organizational structure • Characteristics of environment & technology • Models of organization & system	1. **Organization Design** Formulating & aligning elements of an organizational system. • Concepts of organizational fit & alignment. • Diagnostic & design models for various subsystems that make up an organization at any level of analysis. • Key thought leaders in organizational design. 2. **Organizational research** Field research, content analysis, designing questionnaires, designing change evaluation processes, data collection & analysis; etc. 3. **Systems Dynamics** The understanding of how systems evolve & develop over time. How systems respond to exogenous & endogenous disruptions as well as planned interventions. 4. **History of OD and change:** An understanding of the social, political, economic and personal forces that led to the emergence and development of organization development and change.

4. Research methods/Statistics/ Quantitative techniques • Measures of central tendency • Measures of dispersion • Basic sampling theory • Basic experimental design • Sample inferential statistics 5. Functional Knowledge of Business • Interpersonal communication • Collaboration • Problem Solving • Using New technology • Conceptualizing • Project management	5. Theories and models for change: • The basic action research model • Participatory action research model • Planning model, • Change typologies • Lewin's model, • Transition model and so on

Skills based competencies

Managing the Consulting Process
Analysis/Diagnosis of the system
Designing/Choosing the appropriate interventions
Facilitation & Process Consultation
Developing Client Capability
Evaluating Organizational Change

Future of OD: A Thought.

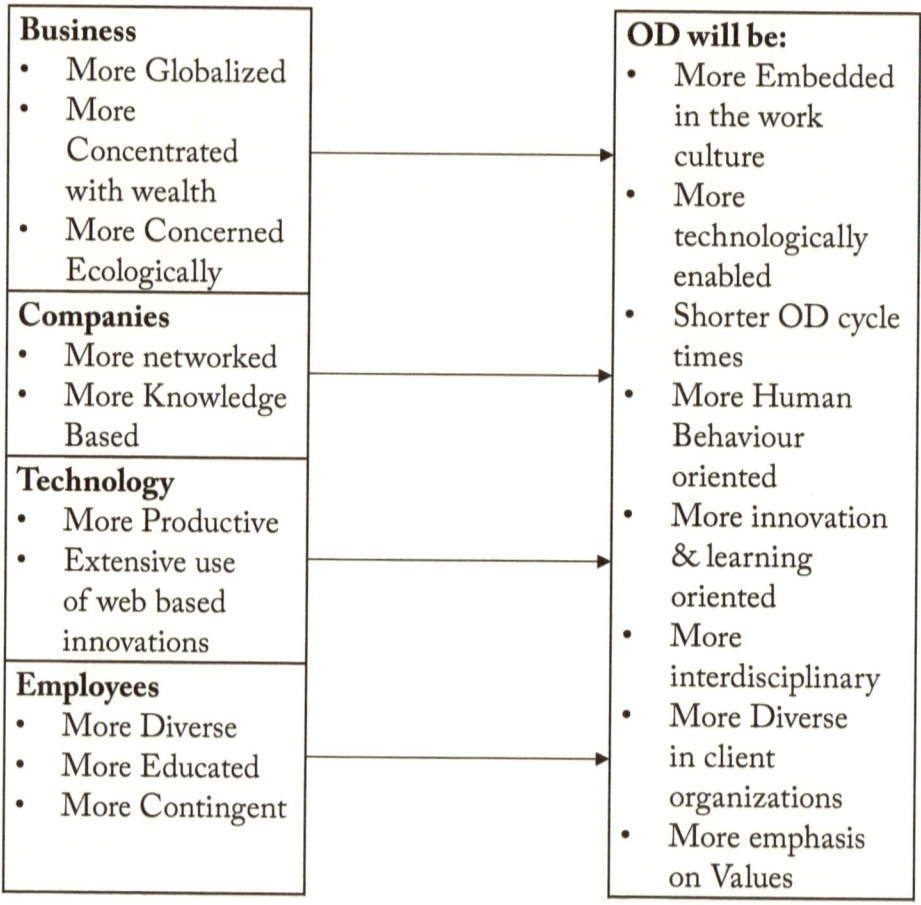

There are several interrelated trends that affect the context within which OD will be applied in near future.

The Chart depicts a thought process and the way business would need to adopt. The practice of OD therefore would be more embedded in the organization's functions.

Although it is increasingly becoming system oriented, the human component however cannot be ignored and will continue to influence the future of the organizations and the way business is done.

CHAPTER 2

An Introduction To Training

Introduction

We live in an age of innovation. Some 25 % of the jobs that exist today were not known some 10 years ago. Bill Gates once made a statement: "In three years, every technology we create becomes obsolete. The only question is whether we'll make them or someone else will." Change is accelerating at a breathless pace. Organizational success will depend on its ability to compete, often within the global economy. Today the markets are merging to form a global economy. There is a lot of flexibility in terms of work place, markets, etc.

As the pace of technology & changes increase, organizations are required to train the employees, clients or customers increasingly more often, more efficiently & at a lesser cost. In today's business world, people are the critical difference & sometimes the only difference between organizational success & failure. Training is the primary way to develop the people in firms. Organizations are also investing more in training. Human skills are more frequently the most important resource an organization has to offer. All the resources are transferable or easily copied by competitors, but an individual is a unique resource & training is the key to making the best use of individual skills.

Training is providing information & direction in a planned & structured manner to employees on how to accomplish a specific task related to organizational needs & objectives. Training should lead to permanent behavioral change & measurable improvement in Job performance. Although training is a single event, in reality it is planned continuous process which begins with identifying the learning that is required.

Any training may include 3 types of data:

1. **Facts and figures:** This is pure data & information. In terms of training, this could be technical know-how, general instructions, code of conduct, employees' policy & likes. Such information could be shared by use of sessions or even when the employees

are on their respective Jobs or a manual of such information as deemed necessary could be provided to the employees.
2. **Policy and procedures:** This provides detailed information about how to do accomplish a specific task. This may account for likes of how to prepare a specific report, approach a customer, production related know-how etc.
3. **Concepts and knowhow:** This includes why as well as how. This gives context to the content & a more detailed explanation citing reasons for a particular behavior expressed while on duty.

Categories of training:

Training in any organization could be classified into 3 categories:

1. Induction
2. Functional Skills
3. Career Development

1. Induction is a training that relates to providing the information (knowledge, but not usually skills) necessary to function in an organizational setting. It is usually for the new recruits. Typical orientation includes history of the organization, its philosophies, structure & Position in the industry, the vision, work rules, leave policies, benefits & other information of general nature that could be used on daily basis by the employee.

2. Functional Skills provides knowledge & skills necessary to perform a specific task or the work for which the individual was hired for. When a skilled or experienced worker is hired, such training is not required or required for a lesser extent. The skilled hire may require Lead central project management Lead central project management knowing the organizational way of doing the tasks.

3. Career Development prepares the employee to take up newer responsibilities. This is for their advancement in their job & in a way in their career. This also counts for their personal growth. It may include formal training in the organization, Job rotation, external training etc. Development activity is not generally tied up to specific positions in an organization but relates to broader skills & concepts necessary for the growth within the organization.

Training versus Formal education

The key comparison in learning in an academic setting & the training in an organization is mentioned in the table below:

Criteria	Academic based	Workshops in organization
Faculty Credentials	Pure Academic; Sometimes a PhD is a must.	Skill or knowledge in the relevant subject regardless of the academic achievements; also interpersonal communications is very important.
Scope/Content	Usually broad & theoretical. Some areas as sciences may have practical elements.	Focused & application oriented. Deals mostly with facts & procedures; rarely with concepts.
Objective	Knowledge based & rarely Job or task oriented learning occurs	Although training is given in knowledge or skill area, the major concern is performance in the Job.
Duration	Time frame is longer compared to a training program.	Time frame is pretty short
Evaluation	Graded using scales or scores or ranks	Generally not graded; but the overall outcomes could be success or failure

Purpose	**For career & employment reasons or self satisfaction**	Required by the employer in order to support the organizational needs.
Student	**Individuals**	Groups or teams may be the constituent units
Study Material	**Comprehensive textbooks & research**	Faculty made materials; cases, sometimes extracts from books or web based materials.

Role of Trainer

The typical training job requires an individual who understands the skills & knowledge being taught & who has effective interpersonal communication skills. Most trainers also need to learn how to identify the needs of the client organization, design training, using media to deliver the training & measuring the results of the training delivered.

ASTD (Formerly American Society for training & development) has listed some major areas of expertise needed by trainers.
- Career Planning & talent management
- Coaching
- Managing organizational Knowledge
- Managing the learning function
- Facilitating organizational change
- Measuring & evaluating
- Delivering training
- Improving human performance
- Designing learning

To develop expertise in these areas, the facilitator needs to build on a foundation of personal, interpersonal , business & management competencies.

Training Cycle

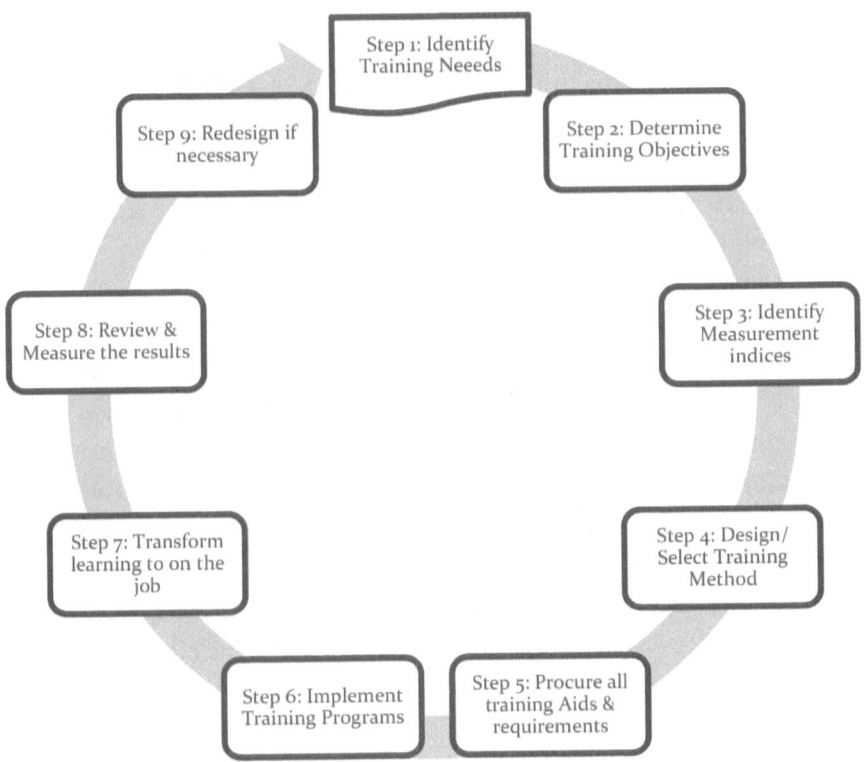

Before initiating any further action the trainer must seek answers to the following questions
1. Does a problem exist?
2. If it does, is it a problem which concerns training?
3. Can training help?
4. What should the training process seek to achieve?

In any case the trainer should look for some obvious symptoms like
- A mismatch between the policies & practices
- Staff being unaware of their duties & failing to adhere to the organization's policies.

- Discriminatory & sensitive acts are prevalent; training is required to prevent such acts in future.
- Organization's/Department's/SBU's targets are not being met.

Adult Learning Styles

As a student, one can recall the classroom sessions where the teacher determined the content, structure, sequence, presentation & evaluations. Most of the formal education follows this structure. However there were certain curious kind of students who used to find their own ways of learning rather than following the path shown by the teachers. There is a visible mismatch between the teaching style of the instructor & the learning style of the learner. Learning can take place only if both these styles are successfully integrated. Early childhood focuses on body of fundamental rules & content rules. When these fundamentals are mastered, the student is ready for the higher order learning.

The table overleaf expresses the various learning styles. Here Andragogy refers to study of teaching adults while Pedagogy is for the study of teaching children.

Various Adult learning Styles

Dimension	Pedagogy	Andragogy
The Need to Know	Must learn what the Teacher teaches. Need not know the relevance of "Taught" in their lives.	Need to know why they need to learn.

Learners Self Concept	Learner is a Dependent Person Teacher is responsible for all decisions A learner is submissive to the teacher's directions.	Learner is self Directed Learner is responsible for his/her learning Learner enjoys equality with the teacher.
The role of experience	Learner's experience is of Little value Teacher is the one who knows all.	Learners have a quality of experience. Learners are the sources of Learning for each other. Experience is also responsible for preconceived notions.
Readiness to Learn	Learners are told what & when to learn. Readiness is largely related to age.	Adults are ready when they have needed to know. Readiness is largely related to a real life problem.
Orientation of Learning	Subject centered orientation. Content is sequenced logically.	Life centered, task centered or problem centered orientation to learning Content is sequenced around life situation.
Motivation to Learn	Learners are exclusively motivated by external motivators like Grades, parental pressures or Teacher's approval or disapproval	Primarily from internal motivators like self actualization, esteem, recognition etc.

How do Adults learn?

Some Concepts:

Perceptions: Some Preconceived notion or idea about any particular theory, person or object. The perceptions may hinder learning as they block the path of unlearning in order to give space to the newer concepts.

Context: If information is given without any context, it will be difficult to understand. What is clear to you may be terribly unclear to the trainees. Hence it is very necessary to provide with the background for any point that needs explanation. It is really necessary for the person receiving instructions to know where the information fits into the bigger picture.

Chunks: For maximum learning & retention of knowledge, the information must be given in chunks.

Take an activity:

- Write down the following words in a paper:
  Pen, Mobile, Sloth, File, Juicer, Elephant, Paper, telephone, Blue, Printer, Red, Cow, Stapler, Yellow and Paperweight
    - I believe that you cannot put them in sequence.
- Now classify the data & create CHUNKS of the information
    - Stationery: File, Paper, Paperweight, Pen, Printer, Stapler
    - Electronics: Mobile, Juicer,
    - Animals: Cow, Sloth, Elephant
    - Colours: Red, Yellow, Blue
- This makes the learning easy.

Sequencing: The way we sequence the delivery of the information can also have a huge impact on the results.

Amount: The amount of information we give can also have an impact on the results. If we give out too much irrelevant information, the real message gets buried.

The Nine Principles of Adult learning:

The term learning has several interpretations, but is generally accepted as a change in the behavior or attitude.

The below mentioned principles are basically same as those put forward by any 'methods instructions course'.

1. **Recency-** The law of Recency tells that the things that are learnt last are those that are best remembered by the participant. This applies in two separate areas of learning. First, it applies to the content at the end of the session. Secondly, this applies to the things that are most fresh in the minds of the participants. For the first application it is necessary for the trainer to summarize frequently. Trainers should place review sections in their plan in order to keep the vital content fresh.
2. **Appropriateness-** The training tools & aids, case studies, & other settings must be appropriate to the needs of the participants. Participants would lose motivation if the tools do not match the concepts or skills to be learnt.
3. **Motivation-** The law of motivation says that the participants must be ready to learn, must be willing to learn & have a strong reason to learn. If they have a sense of learning, they will excel.
4. **Primacy-** The law of primacy states that the skills taught first are learnt faster & retained for a longer time.
5. **2 Way communications-** training process involves communication between the trainer & trainees.
6. **Feedback-** Both the facilitator & the participant need the information from each other. The facilitator needs to know that participants are keeping pace & the participants need the feedback on their standard of performance.
7. **Active Learning-** Participants learn more when they are actively involved in the process.
8. **Multi Sense Learning-** Learning is faster & more effective if all the participants use more than one of their five senses.
9. **Exercise-** things are remembered easily if they are repeated. This is also called the principle of over learning.

CHAPTER 3
Strategic Perspective Of Training

Strategic Perspective of Training

Strategic training means that training plans take into account long-term organizational goals and objectives. Example of these goals might include the development of new or better products, operating with fewer people or expanding to a global market. Strategic training efforts are typically initiated by top management- the chief executive officer or the chief learning officer.

Developing a workforce with core competencies is strategic. Core competencies are the knowledge, skills. Abilities and attitudes of the organization has deemed critical to long term success, such as creative thinking and problem-solving, leadership and visioning and self development. The development of core competencies not only contributes to organizational goals but also adds to personal mastery. Such core competencies become the foundation for specific job skills.

For example: assume that a large U.S. corporation is in the midst of expanding its business to include distributors in Mexico. In its global central office, workers must be relatively fluent in Spanish and should be knowledgeable about Mexico's history and culture. A training programme teaches these language skills and cognitive skills would be considered strategic as individual's success in such a training programme would be paramount to the organizations being successful in this new global environment.

Providing training programmes for partners, suppliers and customers may also be considered strategic. For example: Motorola, Anheuser-Busch and Harley Davidson not only invest between 3 and 5 percent of their payroll on training, they extend their training through their entire customer and supply chains. Such efforts address the very nature of an organization and are easily labeled strategic and thus appropriately linked to organizational goals.

Pyramid Approach to Strategic Planning

CHAPTER 4
Training Need Analysis

Introduction

Training needs analysis is a term being used often but unfortunately many people do not fully understand its meaning. So, what does it mean? To answer this question we first need to understand what is meant by a training need. A training need exists when there is a gap between what is required of a person to perform their duties competently and what they actually know which enables them to do so. A training needs analysis is the method of determining whether a training need exists, and if it does, what training is required to fill the gap.

Generally, the training needs analysis will highlight the subject matter needing to be covered during the instruction. The knowledge gained by the participants will help to increase their level of ability and allow them to perform their tasks at an acceptable level.

An example of such a situation may be where a company purchases a number of new computers for its warehouse operation. None of the staff in the warehouse has used this type of computer system or software before- in fact it will be the first time computers will be used in the warehouse. This is a very simple example of a training need. The training needs analysis in this case is simply a matter of identifying such an obvious need.

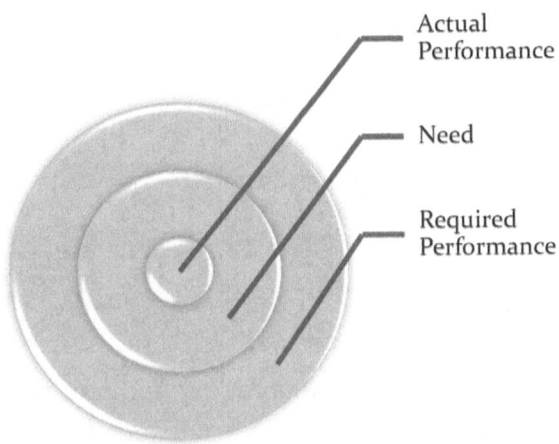

Changing the above example, let us now say that the company did have some computers in the warehouse before, but a different type, and that some of the staff did have some experience with them. In this situation we can again see a training need, but the solution is not as obvious. By carrying out a training needs analysis we would be able to target the group to be trained and also find out what training was required.

Training Needs can be identified in any number of areas, and some of the more common indicators are:
- complaints from staff
- complaints from customers/clients
- poor quality of work
- frequent errors
- over handling items
- inadequate recruiting process
- large staff turnover
- performance dates not met
- conflicts among staff
- new equipments/systems

This list is not comprehensive and each organization may have different indicators to show a training need. What is important is that once a training need or gap has been identified, it should be filled.

When we carry out a training needs analysis we are usually interested in collecting the following types of information:
- job roles
- job process
- job problems
- task list
- task frequency
- task difficulties
- task importance

A simple statement that should be applied to any identified performance problem is 'If a person's life depended on them performing a skill and they could do it but they don't, its management problem, if they couldn't do it, it's a training problem. Management problems cannot always be solved by training and may need to be handed back to management to solve.

Identification of Training Needs

Ramesh was the manager of an order processing unit and he had a problem. He was dissatisfied with the performance of his group. They seemed to be taking forever to process essential paperwork. He decided that a time management, training programme would solve the problem.

Ramesh hired a consultant to conduct a 2 day time management programme. All employees attended. The evaluation indicated the course had been well received and the information found useful.

After the course Ramesh expected a change in the speed of processing. Unfortunately it never happened. The paper work continued at the same snail pace. Ramesh was dismayed, he had spent Rs. 40,000 and he was not getting the desired results.

1. **What had gone wrong?**

Ramesh selected and shot his arrow before he set up his target. He aimed his solution into a void, and as a result he got nothing.

2. **What should Ramesh have done?**

Ramesh should have gathered information to help him to identify the **real issue.** This would have helped in customizing the training to the **specific needs.**

An essential step for planning and designing a training programme is to **determine** the objectives of the programme. The **objectives are outcomes of the needs of participants.**

Identification of training need is a **very critical aspect** of the training process.

What is a training need?

Each role requires the role occupant to have a certain level of competence in terms of knowledge, skills & attitudes.

| Expected level of Knowledge, skills & attitudes | **GAP** (Training Needs) | Actual level of Knowledge, skills and attitudes |

The gap between the expected level of competence and the actual level of competence are the training needs.

Why assess training needs?

- To assure your training **addresses the real issues.**
- It helps you to **identify the correct methodology** for achieving best results.
- It gets others to **participate in the process**. This helps them to understand issues.
- Participation and **involvement** leads to **commitment** which in turn accelerates the change process.
- Helps to effectively use resources, like money and time towards focused needs.
- Training needs analysis surfaces issues which **while appearing independent on deeper analysis are inter related.** Systemic assessment of needs provides a platform for designing impactful, integrated training interventions.

Kind of training needs

Training needs may be classified under the following categories:

1. Individual versus group needs
2. Short- term versus long term needs
3. Institutional and formal versus informal needs.

4. Needs which can be met by internal resources versus those to be met by external resources
5. Training needs which can be met by an individual himself versus those which can be met only in the company of others?

A proper assessment of training needs consists in finding suitable answers to the following questions:
1. What kind of information, skills and attitudes are to be imparted………
2. Who are the individuals to be trained…..
3. When i.e. at what stage of an individual's service career is training to be imparted……….
4. How, by what means and by whom should the training be imparted………
5. How long should be the optimum training period…….
6. Where the training should be given i.e. in an outside institution, within department, on the job, etc.…

The appropriate answers are found to the above question "what", 'what', 'who', 'when', 'how', 'how long', and 'where', assessment of training needs becomes a comparatively easy exercise.

Process for training needs identification

Action	Output
Visualize the future	Clarity of where you want to be
Assess your current situation	A clear definition of where you are now
Sort information collected	Will identify gaps, issues that need to be addressed
Share Results	Will involve how do we move forward

Action Plan   Will result in implementation of
                                                action plans

Training Need Identification Methods

Some of the methods of assessing the training needs in organization are:

- Studying new policies/old policies/new objectives in the organization
- Observing what is going on in the organization
- Studying new process/observing training required for new equipments
- Analysis of behavior of people
- Management requests
- Self analysis and self appraisal
- Test or examinations
- Training advisory committees
- Conferences/interviews/informal talks

Three Levels of Training Need Identification

1. Organizational Level identification
2. Post/Designation Level identification
3. Employee Level identification

1. Organizational level identification:

An organization is a group of individuals working towards a common goal or a cause. So, the training function must be in a match with the organization's strategy & goals. The training programs should aim at attaining the objectives of the business. Therefore conducting an organizational need assessment must be the first step in effective needs assessment.

If the organization is planning for an expansion into a new territory, this move requires newer employees. So, the workforce planning must be at its place to tell how many more employees one requires. Again the newer recruits must be trained. Even some of the older employees are relocated to the newer regions. Fair chances these relocations go along with Job enrichment programs. So, even they require training. Thus organizational targets are first place to look for while planning a training program.

2. **Post/designation level identification:**

There should be connection between Organization's strategy and KRA of Post. Furthermore there should be defined Knowledge and set of skills to perform the KRA. These can be done by asking the individuals the performer's perceptions and their superior's perceptions. One can use Questionnaire tool to identify Training need for Post/designation level.

The review can be done yearly but it is ideal to do it if you bring in new technology or change in job.

3. **Employee level identification:**

Here we are comparing the employee with desired performance (in broad approach) or proficiency on each required skill dimension (in narrower approach).

Performance Appraisal:

The first method is based on the actual, current job performance of an employee; therefore, it can be used to determine training needs for the current job. This helps to identify the differences between organization's expectations & the individual's performance. A performance appraisal measures the employee's performance & also tells about the attitude, skills, knowledge &Behavior of the employee. This exposes the areas that require change. The identification comes from the employee or out of the discussion between the employee & the supervisor who prepares the appraisal. Organizations do the appraisal process in a systematic way.

Generally TNI forms a major part of the appraisal system. The needs identified are then collated & suitable training programs are designed.

Career Plans:

The second method, on the other hand, can be used to identify development needs for future jobs. The above title accounts for any kind of promotion like Job enrichment/enlargement, transfers etc. On such events, the information regarding the newer tasks is considered. The changes in content of the Job help the training manager to organize needful training programs for the employee.

Whether the focus is on performance of the job as a whole or on particular aspects of the job, several approaches can be used to identify the training needs of individuals:

Self-Assessment:

It is easily acceptable the one knows well about the training requirements than other. We can structure the thought process through predefined questionnaire or counseling.

Attitude Surveys:

A 360 degree survey can be done for this where superior, subordinates, and customers can review. The end result can be compared with other employees and the person who is getting low ratings has to undergone the training.

Direct Observation:

Based on the Supervisor's observations about the pattern of the working of the employee, some training needs could be identified.

Apart from the above, the suitability of the training program should also be checked.

Training is one of several solutions to employment problems. However, it may not always be the best solution. It is important to determine if training will be effective in its usage.
The Trainer or the HR manager himself cannot exercise the TNA. The support of the line managers is required. The trainer is primarily responsible for the design & the conduct of the suitable training program. If the need identification itself is wrong, the training will be of little use to employees.

In the above context, the Line managers must ask themselves the following questions:

- Do I know the present job description of the subordinate?
- Do I know the problems faced by the subordinate in performing the job tasks & the way the employee deals with them?
- Do I know the subordinate's strengths & weaknesses in relation to the Job performed?
- Do I know how the employee deals with his/her subordinates & colleagues?
- Do I know his/her potential in relation to the organizational needs?
- Have I considered the above-mentioned details while recommending a training program for the subordinate?

The answer from the line manager needs to be in affirmation in order to render the person qualified to provide reliable data for need identification. However, in organizations, the productivity being on stake, Line managers are not able to justify by working out such micro level of details.

TNI could be best done by the immediate supervisor in consultation with the subordinate. Before jumping to training, it should also be verified if the training could yield the desired result. In case if the training cannot bring out the desired result, it should not be recommended & instead some other method should be found out for achieving the desired result.

In many cases, managers & other employees are recommended for training not because of need being identified, but based on their availability. This happens when there is not real need identification & the Line managers seem to have no faith on the training method.

There is a need for free flow of information between the Line managers of each department & training department. The Line managers must take interest & find out which particular employee requires training in a particular area of function.

The nine step Training Needs analysis process

1. Gather data about a job within the organization

2. Develop an understanding of the performance standards applied to that job

3. Measure the performance that is occurring

4. Determine differences between standards and performance

5. Calculate the cost of that disparity. If it's low, stop. If it's substantial, go on

6. Assess employee levels of skill and knowledge about the job

7. Analyze the gap between job requirements and the current or potential employee's level of performance.

8. Propose training (or other) solutions appropriate to eliminating the differences between requirements and employee performance.

9. Implement the solutions and see if that solves the problems. If not, then repeat the process.

Needs Analysis Model

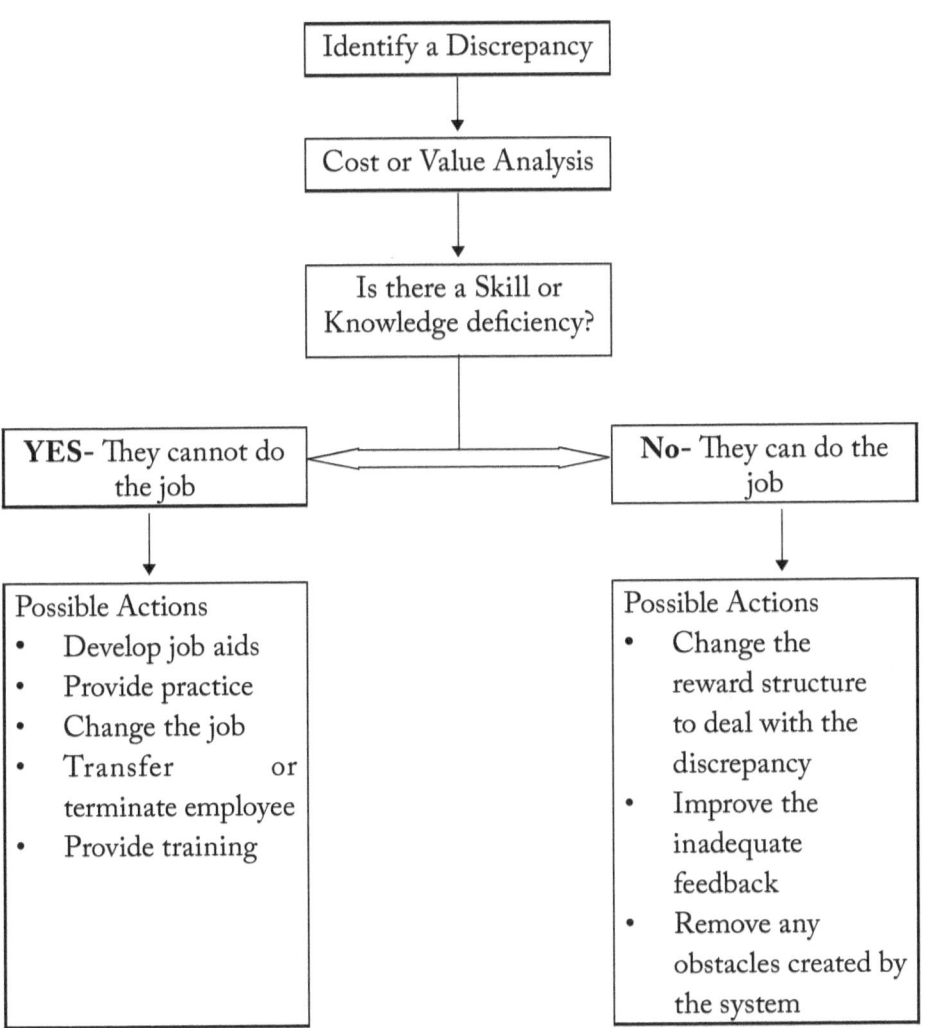

CHAPTER 5
Training Design

Training Objective

Planning a training intervention without setting clear objectives is like a rebel without a cause. In order to ensure that training hits the bulls eye you need to determine the following.

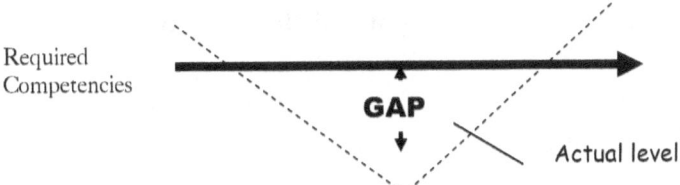

- Why does this gap exist?
- What will be needed to bridge this gap?

Knowledge   *Skills*   *Attitude*

An assessment of needs in terms of knowledge, skills and attitude will help you to create your training objectives. A clear training objective will facilitate the
- Designing of the programme
- Training approach
- Preparing the training material

Training Objective

An architect cannot build a house unless he knows the specific requirements. An interior designer can choose material etc. only after he understands what effects are desired to be achieved. Similarly a facilitator needs to understand the needs and desired outputs to be able to create powerful lasting interventions.
Points to keep in mind while establishing objectives

- Create training objectives in a simple way, remaining focused on the end results.
- Training objectives should clearly state in specific measurable terms what a participant will be able to do after the training
- Do not promise more than you can deliver E.g. Training will "improve productivity in the organization or change the trainee's attitude" are not deliverable objectives.

Training objectives will fall into one of the three broad categories:

1. **Knowledge**: Acquiring of knowledge/understanding of concepts
2. **Skills**: The practice of new skills or behavior
3. **Awareness**: Explanation of attitudes feelings and preferences.

Training content & Delivery

Designing the Training Program

After identifying training needs and setting clear specific measurable objectives the next critical step in the training process is the design.

Designing the programme would consist of the following steps.
  a. Basic information
  b. Contents
  c. Methods
  d. Sequencing

a. **Basic information**(would mean, gathering information on):
   - Number of participants
   - Background of participants
   - Profile of participants
   - Age
   - Gender
   - Background and previous training experience of participants
   - Familiarity of participants with each other
   - Location of programme
   - Allotted time
   - Budget
   - Residential/non residential
   - Facilitator/trainer expertise

b. **Contents:**
Specific information on
   - Why do the trainees need the training?
   - What do the trainees need to know?
   - How can it be delivered?

Design pre, during and post programme interventions:

c. **Methods:**

To deepen the learning process it is imperative to expose the participant to various learning methods. It is important to remember that different people learn differently. A trainer must incorporate as many modes of learning as possible.

E.g. Visual learners would find learning more enriching when bright charts and innovative videos are used.

Kinesthetic learners learn most with experience oriented exercises.

Auditory learners revel in audio tapes, conversations and exercises where they can listen to each other.

Remember to use as many methods as possible (Case studies, Role plays, Games, Exercises, etc.)

While choosing methods, choose the one where the objectives will be best met. Keep connecting with the participants profile and work experience for best fit.

Always choose methods which are aligned to what the objective is i.e. enhancing knowledge, honing skills or cultivating attitudes.

d. Sequencing

How you sequences your training programme is a critical designing aspects. Typically the process will unfold as follows:

Steps 1

Look at each of the objectives, and categorize your contents into
- Must include
- Nice to include
- Don't really need to include

Give it a good, honest look

Step 2

Keeping the objective in mind, decide how much experiential/hand on time needs to be scheduled.

Step 3

You cannot teach your participants everything they need to know at once. You will need to organize what you are going to do in a systemic manner. You could choose to move from
- Simple to complex
- Highest to lowest priority

You will need to develop an instructional map or plan.

Some tips to remember while designing a training programme

While sequencing
- More gradually from what participants know to what they do not
- Choose powerful training methods
- Make a list of resources you will need simultaneously
- Allocate sufficient time for each session. Be realistic.

Include items which will help the participants to remember what they have learned. Use
- Checklist
- Forms

- Quick reference cards
- Worksheets
- Visual reminders

Designing methods

Overview:

Methods add depth and variety to a training programme. They enhance the learning process. A properly selected, adapted or written, training methods or activity is only as good as how it is introduced, conducted, and processed. These three skills are critical to ensure optimal learning.

The skills of processing is especially critical with experiential activities such as simulations (case studies, role plays and clinics)

There are 3 critical steps for conducting any method effectively.
→ Introducing an activity
→ Conducting an activity
→ Processing an activity

Introducing an activity
- Give a purpose and objective for the upcoming activity
- Rearrange furniture and regroup participants as needed but as smoothly as possible. Wait until everyone is settling before proceeding.
- Elicit information from participants as to what experience or knowledge they already have on the topic.
- Provide definitions of all terms to be used.
- Give directions that not only explain the activity but tell what will happen afterwards. E.g. will the data on the questionnaire be shared and if so, how? Will everyone be paired up to replicate the demonstration that they are about to see?
- Distribute any printed instructions and read them together before starting the activity. If you will be giving only oral directions, be sure to have everyone's attention before starting.

- Answer questions before continuing
- Demonstrate rules or procedure
- If you are using an activity that requires them to participate, always be the first to share to try it out.
- Roam around the room to determine if everyone knows what to do.

Conducting an Activity
- Expect some confusion and/or frustration. Some of this helps to encourage problem solving and learning
- Be available to re-explain the directions
- Stick to your role as the facilitator. Don't try to play a game and also guide it at the same time.
- Be observant at all times as to how individuals and groups are working on the problems, how well they work together and when they need prodding or help from you.

Processing an Activity
- Plan on using about as much time to process an experiential activity as it look to conduct it.
- If you used only some participants to do a demonstration or role play, first ask for feedback from them, then elicit feedback from the observer.
- Prepare and ask questions that:
    → Review or summarize what happened in the activity or what they learned
    → Identify feelings that occurred at different points in their learning experience
    → Identify choices they considered and how they made a particular decision
    → Point out different roles people played during the experience
    → Identify any patterns in the information, behaviors or attitudes
    → Reveal conflicts and other unfinished business
    → Highlight the possibility of trying out alternative behaviors

- Record participants feedback and ideas on the flipchart. Use a participant as recorder to keep you free to lead the discussion.
- Expect difference of opinion and perceptions. Enforce your guidelines on giving each other feedback so all ideas are accepted and personal attacks do not occur.
- Be sure to complete the learning cycle and help participants relate the learning experience back to the lesson's objectives and to their own real situations.
- Ask for feedback on your learning activity so you can evaluate its effectiveness.

Training methods that work

Method 1: Structured warm-up activities

Benefits of using structure activities in the beginning of a training programme are:
- Gets the participants involved right away. They enjoy hands on experiences.
- Increases their energy and interest levels
- Gives an early introduction to a key idea or skill that will be developed later.

Some examples of warm-up activities are:

The quiz

In training courses where facts must be learned, it is essential to "exercise" students with new knowledge. Written tests are fine but remind students of their school days.

A well – devised quiz will appeal and test at the same time.

Suggestions on how to conduct:

- Break group into quiz teams to provoke competition
- Invent different categories of questions like on TV. Game shows.

- Keep scores on imaginatively designed board
- Don't forget the prizes!

Method 2: The presentation

Overview

You will need to make a presentation so participants will have essential background information. While conducting training programmes, facilitators use a combination of facilitation and presentation skills.

Presentations have 2 parts
- Contents
- Delivery

> *For preparing the contents systematically, follow the following six steps:*

1. Define your objectives for the presentation
   Be absolutely clear about your purpose. You should be able to state in one clear sentence what you wish to accomplish.
2. Understand/research your audience
   Research your audience as thoroughly as possible.
3. Research for material
   Having understood the needs, start collecting data and research for the latest and the best. You must categorize your data into
   - Basic information
   - Supplementary information
   - Additional information
4. Structure the presentation
   A good presentation is structured like a train, where the engine represents the introduction of the presentation, the bogies the body of the presentation and the guard compartment the conclusion of the presentation.
5. Select and prepare visual aids
   For each main idea, think about using visual aids that could enhance and support the information being presented.
   You can choose from

- Video
- Films
- Flip charts
- Transparencies
- Killer PowerPoint presentations
- Handouts

6. Give the presentation the final touches
   Make sure:
   - The points are in a logical order
   - Indicate in your notes where and what visual aid you are going to use
   - Indicate where likely questions will be asked.

➤ *Delivery of the presentation*

There are no shortcuts to preparation and practice

Some useful tips:
- Stand before a mirror
- Video tape your presentation
- Tape record your presentation
- Present to colleagues and ask for feedback

Delivering the task:

Having prepared thoroughly, you will not fail. But the extent to which you succeed depends also on what you do on the day.

1. Before you even begin, check that:
   - All your notes, handouts, visual aids etc. are ready for use
   - Any necessary equipment such as a microphone is ready for use
   - Heating, seating, lighting and ventilation are as you require
2. Aim for a good first impression:
   - Wait until everyone is quiet
   - Start with energy and enthusiasm
   - Look your audience in the eyes

- Make your introductory remarks without having to refer to your notes
- Stand still and upright
- Smile and look relaxed, confident and in command
- Make sure your voice gets to the back of the room
3. Speak conversationally:
    - Imagine you are talking to people you know well
    - Speak distinctly and not too fast
    - Use natural pauses and emphasis
    - Look at each individual in turn while you talk
    - Don't preach or talk down to your audience
    - Be light of touch and good humored
    - Be yourself
4. Keep your grip on the audience:
    - Maintain eye contact with your audience
    - Don't bury your head in your notes
    - If you must read from a script, look up as often as you can
    - Watch out for signs of puzzlement or restlessness
    - Respond to any such signs you see
    - Don't accept questions in mid-talk unless you really want to say without embarrassment, that you can't answer that one
    - Say you will discuss it with the questioner afterwards or
    - Invite the audience to offer answer
    - Avoid distractions – over gesturing or pacing about
    - Don't 'er' and 'um' – better to have a moment's silence
    - Watch the time!
5. Finish conclusively
    - Let your audience know the end is in sight
    - Have the exact wording of your final sentences clearly in mind
    - Finish off as vigorously as you began

Suggestion
➢ Never, ever, apologize to your audience for lack of speaking ability.
➢ While making a presentation use all your self-your knowledge, your experience and your body effectively.

Method 3: Reading Materials

Overview:

Reading materials can enhance learning as long as they are relevant and their purpose is clearly understood. The positive impact of training is increased when the reading materials is relevant to participants' own situations, at their reading level and done in conjunction with other learning methods.

Guidelines:
- Select the reading materials
- Introduce the purpose and process
- Guided reading
- Follow up

Method 4: Demonstration

Overview:

Demonstration is a powerful training method because participants utilize all their senses.

Demonstrations bring alive whatever points you are trying to make. Participants can experience an idea or technique.

Guidelines:
- Prepare carefully
- Explain the process
- Step by step
- practice

Method 5: Video and Films

Overview:
Videotapes and films help to simulate interest and motivate participants to try new behaviors.

Steps for using video/film training:

Sr. no.	Steps	How/what
1	Prepare for showing	- Preview and identify the important points you want group members to get from viewing the video or film - Try out equipment and checking lighting levels
2	Provide instructions	- Tell participants what they will see and why - Instruct the group what to do during the film - Tell them what they will do after the film
3	Play the video/film	
4	Present/summarize major points	- Discuss - Summarize the key points you want group members to retain from the video/film

Method 6: Note-Taking

Overview:

Whether or not you provide directions or handouts to participants for taking notes, many will do so automatically. These people may be the kind of learners who need to first hear the information, see it in any visual aids you provide and then see it again in the form of notes. Other participants find note-taking a nuisance or unnecessary and seem to be able to listen and learn.

Guidelines:
1. Prepare a handout
   - Title the handout

- Use bold type heading and leave plenty of space for notes to be taken
- Add any heading footnotes or reference

2. Using the handouts
    - Let the participants know if you are providing a handout on which they can take notes… before they start taking notes
    - Explain the purpose for taking notes.

Method 7: Discussion

Overview:
Discussion is probably used most frequently by trainers. However, it isn't learned quickly. The art of questioning takes lots of preparation and practice.

Discussion between the facilitator and participants and those among participants are useful because learners can take a more active role.

Questioning skills:
Questions play a major role in facilitating discussions. Questions are used to:
- Determine what participants know already
- Invite participation and involvement
- Provide you with feedback

There are three skills associated with the questioning process.
- Asking questions of the participants
- Handling their answers to your questions
- Responding to their questions

Asking questions:
Effective questioning means:
- Selecting the right type of question
- Phrasing it to elicit responses
- Directing appropriately

Handling answers to questions:
- Use positive reinforcement for correct answers
- Acknowledge the effort of the respondent, regardless of whether the answer was right or wrong
- Minimize potential embarrassment for wrong or incomplete answers.

Responding to Questions:
- Provide the answer yourself
- Redirect the question back to the person
- Defer the question

Method 8: Questionnaires

Overview:
Questionnaires help gather information on a particular, subject. Questionnaires can measure a person's level of knowledge, attitudes or performance. The questionnaires can also be used for self assessment by the individual who filled it out.

The participants' role is passive but can become more active if combines with another method like the fishbowl or discussion.

Guidelines to remember while using a questionnaire
- Determine your purpose
- Utilizing a questionnaire
- Follow up

Method 9: Case Studies

Overview:
The case study is a printed description of a problem situation with sufficient details for participants to determine appropriate action they might take. A case study simulates reality, drawn upon participants' experiences and knowledge and involves them more actively in the learning process and forces them to apply theory to practice.

Guidelines:
- Review your sources for an appropriate case study that fits your objectives, as needed, adapt the details of the case study or write a case that fits your participants problems or those of the organization
- Divide the participants into groups of four to six
- Explain the purpose of using a case study and read the directions
- Individuals follow the directions, read each case and rank the alternatives responses.
- In small groups, participants hold a discussion of their rankings. You may want them to reach consensus on a group ranking or merely hold a discussion on their rationale for their rankings
- Conduct a discussion with the total group.

Method 10: Role plays

Overview:
Role plays are a hand on method for stimulating real life. The role play enacts an incident and gives participants a chance to re-examine their behavior. It allows them the opportunity to practice and experiment with new behaviors, to emphasize different viewpoints, and to receive feedback on their behavior. A role play draws upon the participants' **experiences and knowledge and forces them to apply theory to practice.**

Five types of role plays:
1. Single:
2. Double
3. Reverse
4. Rotation
5. Multiple

Conducting role plays:
- Arrange the room so that everyone can participate fully.
- Explain the purpose and process to be used
- Verbally designate roles or distribute printed descriptions of the roles and observer's handout. Answer any questions.

- Ask for volunteers to play the roles. During the enactment, only intervene if a player is having difficulty, or if you want to reverse or rotate roles.

Processing the role play:
- Always conduct a feedback session that reviews and analyzes what happened in the role play.
- Prepare open-ended questions that cover both content and feelings.
- **Never rush processing the role play. Allow at least as much time for processing the experience as it took to do it originally.**
- Ask participants to reflect upon how this role play fits into their own reality and what they can take from the exercise back to their lives.

Overcoming resistance to role playing:

Since many people tend to resist role playing (including many trainers), you need to take the following into account:
- Call it by another name, like "Simulation" or "reality playing"
- Use the role playing method later in your training design when participants are more at ease
- Set ground rules so that the players feel safe and reassured that the facilitator will be protecting them from inappropriate feedback
- Introduce the role play without fanfare but clearly explain the purpose and process that will be used.
- Starts out with the multiple role-playing so everyone is involved.
- Ask for volunteers to role play rather than selecting the players (Unless the problem emerged from a particular participant)
- Don't use players who will be inhibited by each other due to their job roles or previous conflicts.
- Focus the process questions on the objectives of the lesson. Also give feedback using the role player's the name and not their real name.

Method 11: Games and other structured activities

Overview:

Games are another form of simulation but generally with a more competitive element to them.

In games and structured activities, participants are actively involved and use all their senses, which increase their energy. They help participants learn a concept or key ideas, increases self awareness, provide practice for risk taking or develop a specific skill.

Guidelines:
- Review your sources for an appropriate game or structured activity that fits your objectives
- Prepare the room and divide the participants into the size of the group that the directions call for
- Explain the purpose of activity and review the directions
- Participants complete the exercises, games or activity
- Process the game using questions that tie into the objectives.

Method 12: Group problem solving (Clinic Method)

Overview:

The content of the clinic method is determined by the participant more than any of the other training methods. Participants are very active in the learning experience and have a hand on opportunity to apply theory using this method.

This method requires the more difficult skill of facilitation. It draws upon your ability to listen, observe, question and give feedback.

According to P.N. Singh

Training methods

1. **Training in the field, on the job:**
    - Apprenticeship

- In- plant training
- Craftsmanship Training

2. **Simulating real life situations:**
   - Role playing
   - Business games
   - In- basket training

3. **laboratory training**
   - Sensitivity training – T- group and L-group
   - Transactional analysis

4. **Sampling real life:**
   - Incidents, Case Method/Case Studies

5. **Individualized Training or Counseling:**
   - Practicing specific Skills
   - Reading and written Assignments
   - Postal Tuition
   - Programmed Instruction

6. **Discussion Methods:**
   - Syndicate Method
   - Seminars, Conferences, Colloquium, Symposium

7. **The lecture method:**
   - To give overall view of the subject matter
   - Teaching complex information
   - Participants are in large number

CHAPTER 6
Training Evaluation

"Because a thing seems difficult for you, do not think it impossible for anyone to accomplish."

— Marcus Aurelius

Measuring effectiveness of training

The six myths of measuring training:

Myth	Reality
1. 'evaluation and measurement are done at the end of trainings' end to determine if the programme was successful"	• Evaluation and measurement should begin before the programme starts. • Baseline data is needed to find the impact of training. • Identifying the measures upfront, will enhance the effectiveness of learning.
2. 'You really cannot measure the results of training efforts. You either believe in it, or you don't.	• It is possible to measure impact of any programme. Only creativity, time and expenses limit it. • The larger the training effort, the more significant the evaluation. Small programmes may not justify full-scale measurement. • The real question is "To what degree is it reasonable and worthwhile to measure the impact?
3. "Measurement only works for skill based programmes"	• To measure "hard skills" time, output, quality and cost are used, for "soft skills" climate/culture can be used. • Measuring "soft skills" needs thorough planning and observation.

4. "Measurement is the responsibility of the training or HR Department."	• "Who is responsible for training" is the key question. It is a team effort between departments. • Linking training objectives to business objectives creates joint responsibility for success. • Team effort builds commitment.
5. "Management hasn't asked for measurement or evaluation.'"	• It helps to be proactive. If the training is not successful, one will be held responsible anyway.
6. "I don't want to open myself up to more work or even unnecessary criticism"	• Continuous improvement cannot take place without measurement and self-examination • Without a continuous improvement focus, the departments become less-than-competitive and eventually become obsolete.

Training Evaluation: Result Based Approach

Objectives
- To examine the need for developing result based approach for evaluation of training
- To understand different levels of evaluation and different issues involved in each step of evaluation

When HRD Becomes a True Business Partner
- HRD must be integrated into overall strategy and operational framework of the organization
- Partnership must be established with key operating managers

- There must be comprehensive measurement and evaluation process for the contribution of HRD
- Some progress is seen in integrating HRD into overall strategy & active partnership of operating managers in HRD efforts
- But not similar progress in the area of measurement & evaluation

Needed a Change & Do Evaluation
- It just makes good economic sense
- More information is available
- Increased scrutiny of HRD budgets
- Pressure from the top to make contribution
- Professionalism & Peer pressure
- Self satisfaction
- Survival

Result – Based Approach
- It represents a philosophy and practice that emphasize results
- Characteristics
- Programs are not usually undertaken unless tangible results can be measured
- Program design includes at least one method of evaluation
- Each HRD staff should have some responsibility for evaluation

Characteristics
- Management is involved in all phases of the process
- A proactive effort is under way to increase management commitment
- A comprehensive evaluation plan is in place
- Participants understand their role to achieve results
- Programs are connected to strategic initiatives

Purposes and Uses of Evaluation
- To determine success of the program
- To identify strengths and weaknesses
- To decide the appropriateness of program as a solution
- To compare costs & benefits

Purposes and Uses of Evaluation...
- To identify successful trainees
- To reinforce major points made to trainees
- To decide prospective trainees
- To market future programs
- To establish a data base

Level based models of Training Evaluation

The Kirkpatrick Four Level Approach
- Reaction:
    - Measures trainees feelings & thoughts about the program
- Learning
    - Measures the extent of learning occurred because of the program
- Behavior
    - Measures the extent of translation of learning KSA into improved behavior on the job
- Results
    - Measures organizational improvement such as cost savings, output changes, quality changes etc

Kaufman Five Levels Model
1a Enabling
   Availability of qualitative human, financial, and physical resources inputs necessary for training
1b Reaction
2 Acquisitions
3 Applications
4 Organizational output
5 societal outcomes
   - Examines the extent of client and societal responsiveness, consequences and pay offs

The CIRO Model
- Context evaluation
  - Obtaining & using data about the current operational levels
    - Immediate objectives: KSA required to change
    - Intermediate objectives; changes in work behavior
    - Ultimate objective: deficiency elimination
- Input evaluation
- Reaction evaluation
- Outcome evaluation

CIPP Model
- Context evaluation
  - Needs assessment & analysis.
    - Assists in forming goals
- Input evaluation
  - What resources and how they are used
    - Helps in program design
- Process evaluation
  - How learning took place
    - Guides implementation
- Product evaluation
  - Outcomes, helps in review decisions

The Philips Five level ROI Framework
- Reactions & planned Actions: Measures reactions & outlines specific plans for implementation
- Learning: Measures KSA changes
- Job Applications: Measures change in behavior on the job & specific application of training material
- Business Results: Measures business impact of the program
- Return on Investment: Measures monetary value of results & costs per program

Understanding levels of Training Evaluation

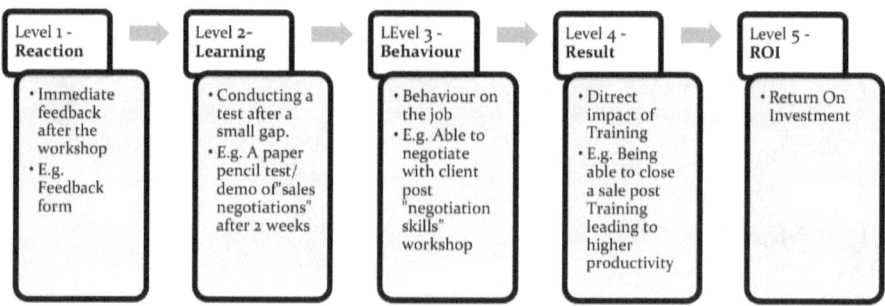

Level 1
Areas of Level 1
- Progress with objectives
- Program content
- Sequence of the content
- Instructional materials
- Pre-training material
- Assignments
- Methods of delivery
- Facilitator
- Facilities
- Planned improvements

Questionnaire
- Open ended questions
- Check list
- Two way questions
- Multiple-choice questions
- Ranking

Questionnaire Design

- Determine the information needed
- Select the type(s) of questions
- Develop questions
- Test the questions
- Finalize the questionnaire

Uses of Reaction Data
- Monitoring customer satisfaction
- Identifying strengths and weaknesses
- Evaluating facilitators
- Evaluating facilities
- Evaluating planned improvements
- Linking with follow up data
- Marketing programs

Limitations
- Subjective, based on the feelings at the time of testing
- Participants may be too polite or too rude
- A good rating is no assurance that participants will practice what has been taught

Useful administrative Guidelines
- Keep responses anonymous
- Have a neutral person collect forms
- Provide a copy in advance
- Explain the purpose
- Explore an ongoing evaluation
- Allow ample time for completing the form

Level 2

Classification
- Based on medium
    - Paper pencil test, simulations, actual piece of work and computer based test
- Based on test design

- Oral exams, essay test, objective tests, norm-referenced test, criterion-referenced test and performance testing

Measuring Learning with Tests
- Norm –referenced tests
    - Compare trainees with each other rather than to specific instructional objectives
- Criterion –referenced test
    - An objective test with a predetermined cut-off score for specific instructional objectives
- Performance testing
    - Allows trainees to exhibit a skill that has learned in the program

Design and Administration of Performance test
- The test should be a representative sample of program
- Each stage should be thoroughly planned
- Through and consistent instructions are necessary
- Procedure should be developed for objective evaluation

Measuring Learning with Simulation
- This involves construction and application of a procedure or task that models activity for the program is conducted
- They can provide accurate evaluation if the performance in simulation is objective & can be clearly measured
- Simulation techniques
    - Electrical/mechanical simulation, task simulations. In-basket etc

Measuring Learning with Less-Structured Activities
- When level 3 evaluation is planned, it's not critical to have a comprehensive level 2 evaluation
- So some less structured evaluation
- Self assessment
    - Purpose should be explained, Anonymous, explanation in case of unsatisfactory
- Instructor assessment

- Check list

Administrative Issues
- Consistency
- Monitoring
- Scoring
- Reporting

Using Level 2 Data
- Providing individual feedback
- Improving training program
- Evaluating instructors

Level 3

Job Application – Trainee Characteristics
- Ability to learn
  - Aptitude & specific intelligence
- Motivation to learn
  - WIIFM, belief in training, perceived need for KSA improvement, perceived back to job situation
- Attitude
  - Job satisfaction, low organizational commitment, intention to leave
- Personality
  - Initiative, *Openness to experience*, extraversion, agreeableness, *conscientiousness*

Needs Assessment
- No needs assessment
- Improper needs assessment
- Ignoring needs while nominating

Training Design and Delivery
- Course content & sequence
- Identical elements

- General principles
- Methodology

Program outcomes
- Reactions
- Learning
- Retention

Back on the Job - Trainee
- Ability to transfer (self efficacy)
- Intention to transfer (WIIFM & perceived support)
- Initiation
- Partial transfer
- Conscious maintenance
- Unconscious maintenance

Back on the Job - Transfer Climate
- Organizational policies and practices
- Extent of encouragement or otherwise to apply
- Consequences when applying

Data Collection Methods: Follow up Questionnaire
- Broad Areas of Data
  - Action plan implementation
  - Use of program materials
  - KSA application
  - Frequency of application
  - Measurable improvements
  - Improvements linked to program
  - Monetary impact
  - Barriers
  - Enablers

Data Collection Methods: Follow up Interviews
- Can be conducted by HRD staff, participant's supervisor or external agency

- Possibility of detailed information when used probing technique
- But time consuming and requires training to ensure consistency

Data Collection Methods: Follow up Focus Groups
- A small group discussion conducted by an experienced facilitator
- When quality judgments are subjective, group judgments are better than single
- Inexpensive and quickly conducted
- Think of planning it when information cannot be collected adequately with simple, quantitative methods

Data Collection Methods: Observation
- The observer may be HRD staff, participant's supervisor, or external
- Behavior check list
- Delayed report method
- Video recording
- Audio monitoring

Data Collection Methods: Action Planning
- Detailed action steps
- Developing action plans:
    - Determining the areas of action
    - Writing the action items
    - How much time will it take
- What on-the-job improvements have been realized
- Are the improvement linked to the program

Data Collection Methods: Performance Contract
- Written agreement between a participant and his/her supervisor in which participant agrees to improve performance
- It is in the form of a project to be completed
- It spells out what is to be accomplished, when and with what results

Data Collection Methods: Monitoring Performance Data
- Enables to measure performance in terms of output, quality, costs, time and satisfaction
- Consider existing data base and reports
- If not, develop additional record keeping system

Appropriate Post-program Data Collection Methods

Method	Level 3	Level 4
Follow up Questionnaires	*	*
Observation	*	
Interviews with participants	*	
Follow up focus groups	*	
Action planning	*	*
Performance contracting	*	*
Performance Monitoring		*

Selecting the Appropriate Method
- Type of data
- Participant time
- Supervisor time
- Costs
- Disruption of normal work activities
- Accuracy

PART- II
Evaluate Training and Development

CHAPTER 1
Concept, Definition and Need for Evaluation

Introduction

In this era of globalization & the emerging market economy & competition, the role of Human resource Development gains significance. Companies big & small have to sustain & grow by enhancing their competitive capability. India has to make a transition from domestic to international business. National training policy calls for spending 1.5 % of wage bill on training.

The tenth five year plan aims at step up of GNP from 5.5 % to 8%. Mega training challenge warrants showing training as an investment for growth rather than cost.

As long as training remained as an act of faith, no need was felt to evaluate its results. The need to demonstrate returns of investment on training resulted in obtaining feedback from the participants. Since the method of self reporting was liable to personal biases, other methods of evaluation evolved over the time. The nature & kind of feedback obtained through evaluation is thus dependent upon one's understanding of the concept of evaluation, its purpose & the methodology adopted.

Concept

Evaluation literally means the assessment of value or worth. It would simply mean the act of judging whether or not the activity to be evaluated is worthwhile in terms of set criteria.

However in the field of training, evaluation has traditionally been taken to include not only the assessment of value, but also the collection & analysis of information on the basis of which the assessment is to be made. Therefore, the concept of evaluation incorporates investigation before & after training as well as during training because one cannot assess training efforts unless something about the before & the after training situation is known.

Definition

Dictionary defines evaluation as *"getting to know the VALUE of something"*.

Hamblin (1970) defined evaluation of training as:

"Any attempt to obtain information (feedback) on the effects of training programme and to assess the value of training in the light of the information for improving further training."

Bramley (1966) writes, *"Evaluation of training is a process of gathering information with which to make decisions about training activities."*

CHAPTER 2
Role of Evaluator

Role of Evaluator

Evaluation is not mono-acting by the evaluator. Role of the evaluator has to be based on sound working relationship with those directly and indirectly involved in training. Mostly it is the trainer or sometimes if the training manager is also the trainer and the evaluator he/she is **to interact with:**

i) The trainees;
ii) The trainee's managers to whom they report;
iii) The other training faculty;
iv) Those responsible for providing the training budget like the HRD policy makers of some members of the company's top team.

In this context, the evaluator has to:

a) Be acceptable to those others;
b) Possess the skill of getting involvement and commitment of others;
c) Have interpersonal sensitivity and trust for frank sharing of feedback;
d) Encourage understanding and selling the benefits of evaluation.

Sometimes assuming the role of evaluator as one who has to just receive feedback, a researcher or a fresher is attached to the trainer to carry out the end-of-the-course evaluation. This fresher may have the expertise of designing and developing evaluation tools and techniques but would be insufficient in promoting utilization of evaluation results.

An evaluator's role involves achieving commonality of purpose amongst the trainers, the evaluators, the sponsors and the end users of training.

CHAPTER 3
Stages of Evaluation

Introduction

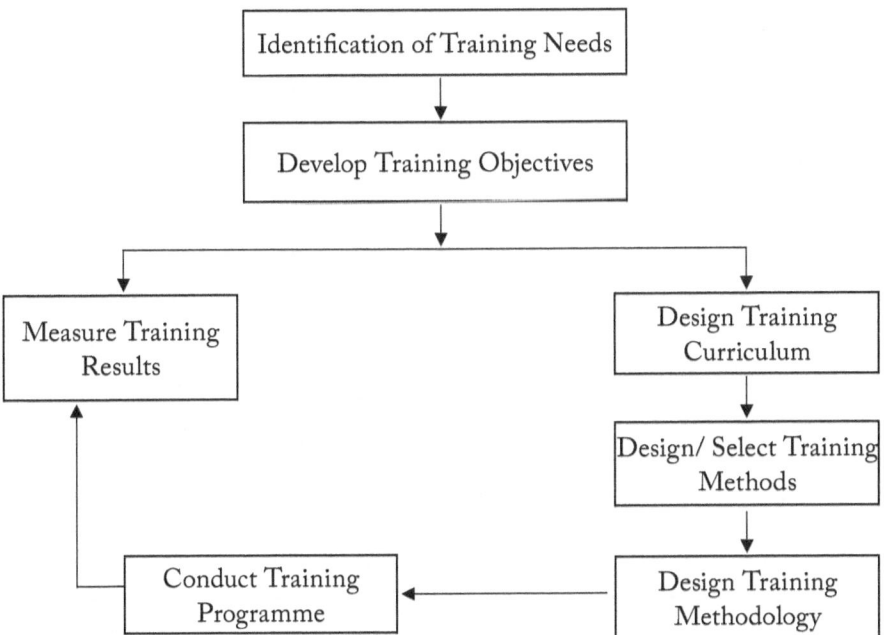

The most common question posed to a trainer at the end of the training cycle is "How effective was the training programme/course"? How does the trainer conclude whether those trained?
- Are better informed and equipped for their jobs?
- Are better able to perform better after training?
- Are able to utilize that training for improving their performance?

Especially when the results of training do not accrue immediately after training and take longer to manifest itself, yet others may not be subtle and not very visible whereas those visible may not be easily measurable.

To enable the trainer to answer these questions to the satisfaction of the customer/client (external training) or the top management o the company (internal training), the evaluator should know 'when' & 'what' to evaluate.

This chapter deals with the methods of evaluation at different stages of training.

Based on the criteria and approach to evaluation many authors have suggested evaluation interventions at different stages of the training cycle.

Level	Reay	Kirkpatrick	Hamblin	Virmani & Premila	Warr
0	-	-	-	-	-
I	Trial phase	-	-	Pre-training context	Context
II	Ongoing phase	-	-	Training input	Input
III	Final phase	Reaction	Reaction	Post training reaction	Process
IV	-	Learning	Learning	Learning	Outcome
V	-	Behaviour	Job behaviour	Job Improvement Plan	Immediate outcome
VI	-	Results	Functioning	On the job	Intermediate outcome
VII	-	-	-	Follow up and transfer	Ultimate outcome
VIII	-	-	-	-	-

Typologies of Evaluation

The above exhibit shows the similarities & dissimilarities in the stages and in terminology of evaluation described by 7 authors. A brief description of typologies is given here.

David Reay's Approach to Evaluation:

David Reay has divided evaluation into three stages:

- I. The Trial Phase.
- II. The Ongoing Phase
- III. The Final Phase

I. **The Trial Phase:** The trial phase is the early tentative phase of development. The evaluation process at this phase comprises of:
- (A) Development Stage involves an informal trial of a sample set of materials, exercises or activities. Being at the very initial stage, if the material is not approved, one can modify, without incurring too much cost.
- (B) Pilot Testing is the second stage of the trial phase. It is a more refined operation and tells the evaluator whether the training being evaluated is suitable for the target population. Under normal working conditions pilot testing even if done on a small sample should be representative to ensure accuracy.

Note: B is confirmation of (A) above.

II. **The Ongoing Phase:** At this phase Reay divides evaluation into two sections.
- (a) Validation is used to measure the effectiveness of a whole training design.
- (b) Formative evaluation is the monitoring of the effectiveness of different aspects of training on a continuous basis with a view to modification.

III. The Final Phase: Ready also calls it the summative phase as it takes place at the end of training events. It looks back on the training process and its outcome, and looks forward to fresh needs and new training initiatives.

Virmani and Premalla's Model of Evaluation:

According to the authors, training constitutes a five stages system. The first stage is the period before training during which the trainees have expectations from the course. The second is the teaching and learning stage and the third is after training when back on the job, the trainees are supposed to integrate training with their job performance.
1. Pre-Training Evaluation
2. Context and Input Evaluation
3. Post-Training Evaluation
4. Evaluating One the Job
5. Follow-up of evaluation

The three stages model is derived from extensive research in the field of management training and development.
1. Pre-Training Evaluation: To ensure maximum of training it is essential that the training objectives match with the expectations of the trainee and with the needs of the user system of training. This effort towards goal congruence of objectives between the trainer, the trainee and the work requirements become all the more essential for external training programmes.
2. Context and Input Evaluation: Pre-training evaluation not only helps in identifying the training, needs based on the trainees' pre-training profile but also helps trainers to evaluate the inputs and its contribution to achievement of training objectives.
3. Post Training Evaluation:

I. Reaction Evaluation: The participants' impressions about the course in general and about specific inputs in particular are measured during and after the course.

II. **Learning:** Equally important as the trainee's reaction to the course is to measures the degree of learning during training. Based on the research findings, Virmani and Premila have suggested arriving at a learning index with the help of pre-training and post-training score (details later in the chapter).

III. **Job Improvement Plan** (JIP): This is another significant step in post-training evaluation. Evaluation of the trainee's improved performance immediately after training without yet providing him an opportunity to put training into practice is a poser to the evaluator. Except for very specific training situations, the nature and diversity of management tasks and the organizational environment requires trainees' skills to work out the scheme and methodology for transfer of training to the job.

To overcome this problem the researchers have recommended the preparation of an individual action plan called JIP for improving his job-performance subsequent to training. Preparation of JIP was found to stimulate the participants and provided the trainees an opportunity to:

a) Evaluate his learning;
b) Perceive the relevance of the training to his job;
c) Adopt concepts and techniques learnt during the training to his job;
d) Identify favourable and unfavourable conditions in the organization which help or hinder of training to the job and find ways to overcome the hindrances;
e) To get back to his work place with more confidence, commitment and positive attitude towards improving one's job-performance because he carries a concrete action plan with him.

4. Evaluating Transfer of Training to the job: On the job evaluation would help assess the transfer of training to the job. If all the steps suggested at the pre-training stage are carefully carried out it would perhaps facilitate optimal utilization of training. This step is not purely evaluative but is an extension of training process. The JIP

could help the trainee elicit support from the organization, his boss, peers and subordinates for transfer of training to the job; it also helps increase receptivity to new ideas by the trainees' immediate work environment.

5. Follow-up of evaluation: Evaluation at this stage involves monitoring and follow-up of the trainees' performance to assess its contribution to the organisation. It also helps in identifying specific areas where improvements have been affected and in evaluating outcome in cost-benefit terms. The JIP can be used as a reference point to check action steps (a) implemented (b) to be implemented and (c) could not be implemented. It would also identify factors that help and hinder application of learning to the job. This data would provide feedback to the trainer for improving subsequent training.

The post-training evaluation data is fed back into the action research cycle for improving subsequent training steps through pre-training evaluation. The model is thus cyclic rather than beginning and ending at each level.

CHAPTER – 4
Evaluation Methods

Introduction

Stages of evaluation are briefly described in the preceding chapter. There is a wide range of possible methods for each stage. In fact the range of evaluation methods is potentially as wide as the range of training methods. However methods should not be confused with stages. Rather the stages form the template on which the methods would be built. The choice of the correct method or combination of methods for a particular stage depends on the nature of the training objectives, the design and methods of training, and the relationship between the trainers, trainees and their superiors, the fiancées, time and resources available.

However all evaluation methods (with exception of some at the ultimate value stage) are variations of the two themes of watching and asking (Observation and Questionnaire/Interview). The advantages/limitations of these two types of methods are complementary and they may preferably be employed together.

Pre-training evaluation

Identification of training needs

Where does the training department vis-à-vis the line manager comes to focus for identification of training needs. No doubt the individual to be trained is the best judge for his needs but two problems arise in accepting these methods.

One, for achieving good appraisal report, individual may not acknowledge his/her deficiencies (training needs) as this can influence his chances of promotions/or increment.

Secondly, even if an individual identifies the areas, do these really get amalgamated into the training, for example does the training department first conduct a need survey and accordingly select/group trainees into different types of training or does selection/identification of the trainees precede the process of identifying what their training needs are.

The line manager should monitor the performance of his/her staff and identify their strengths and weaknesses. If the deficiencies demand immediate correction then He/she may not even wait to respond to his/her training needs or even go a step further to advice remedial training.

In situations where the training department has not established its specialized function and continues to be attached to the personnel or HRD department would be expected to play a reactive role and respond to the needs as identified by the individual or his/her superiors.

A healthy organizational climate encourages the individual and his boss to discuss and record their areas of performance which need improvement through training. The training department should be able to utilize his expertise in helping the individual and his boss to identify areas of training. Ideally, all the three —the trainer, the individual, and his boss can evolve a more meaningful relationship with each other contributing their own professional expertise involvement and commitment towards the total training cycle. Wherever the line manager/individual lack the information, the trainer can provide guidance and where the manager is not sufficiently motivated to develop his subordinates the trainer can play a major role.

These are some of the proactive methods of identifying training needs. A reactive method identifies a discrepancy as failure to achieve targets, or likes could be traced to knowledge, skill or attitudinal gaps of those performing /supervising the task.

Sometimes training needs get identified when the organizations have to respond to:
- Declining Company image
- Change in technology/product/processes.
- Introduction of new systems or policies or procedures.

Any of these changes may call for change in Knowledge, skills; attitude and some of these changes might require job/task analysis to arrive at specific needs.

Overwhelmed with the process of identification of training needs one should be cautious not to end up attributing all performance gaps to be bridged through training when actually the problem lays elsewhere.

Evaluate Performance Standards

Standards of performance are directly linked to Training needs. While the needs of a trainee are person specific, performance standards are job specific. It identifies the tasks a job involves, including the behaviourally anchored outcome. Organizations use measurements of work outputs. Performance standards identified as KRA's finalized between the individual and his/her superior may focus on:
- Productivity
- Profit
- Achieving Deadlines
- Rejections
- Coping with external pressures
- Work Stoppages
- Amount spent on Overtime
- Machine Downtime
- Accident rate

KRA's could be gathered from the appraisal formats or even from the personnel department.

For behavioural outcome the method of evaluation would include:
- A detailed description of each behaviour
- Method of measuring quality of behaviour

Evaluate Training Objectives

This measures the congruence between trainee's needs and the training objectives. The mismatch arises when training is trainer centered, especially external training, when the trainer determines the objectives of the course and the views of the trainees are rarely sought. Here mailing of questionnaire combined with interview with the line managers who are to sponsor their staff would be most feasible. As regards internal training individual and group discussions with the trainee, his superior and peers would be ideal.

Evaluate Trainee's profile

Trainee's level of knowledge, skills and attitude prior to training forms the baseline for determining the training need and for the post training evaluation. Although this won't be possible for each trainee, but some measure of pre-training knowledge skills and attitude is desirable for comparison against post-training performance.

Input Evaluation

Input evaluation varies depending on the team versus individual approach for designing the curriculum. Committee approach has been found to be fairly successful for input evaluation. Brainstorming session would also help in situations where feedback on the subject is already available.

Evaluation during training

Methods of evaluation during training are mentioned below:

1. Observation:
Trainer's perceptiveness and observation skills cannot be discounted except:
- a) Trainer's bias being personally involved
   In this case the observation data must be quantified on a given format. It can also be checked by more than one observer.
- b) Use of TV camera can be one option but participants may become camera conscious or may overact. Over a period of time, it may become an aid to training by letting the trainees watch their performance and use it for self assessment of their skills.

2. Behaviour Analysis:

Monitoring behaviour during training helps imbibing certain skills and attitudes.

3. Course Audits:

Midway training audits can give feedback for immediate corrections. Audits can be conducted at various durations as towards the end of the day (in case of long term courses) or midway during the course.

Such an audit could have questions as mentioned below:
- What is your learning from the course?
- What contributed to this learning (inputs, trainer, group, own effort)?
- Factors that hindered your learning & methods to overcome them
- Inputs to be deleted/added to make the rest of the training more meaningful.

The data thus obtained should be analyzed and wherever possible, corrective action can be taken.

4. Session Assessment:

Assessment after each & every session is done generally using semantic differential scale, three or five point and the trainee is supposed to tick mark. Here it is more important to be clear why we want the assessment immediately after the session. The negative feedback can be assessed and worked upon immediately.

Precautions for Mid-Course review:

A review during the training activity can help the trainer focus on the objectives. However, the trainer ought to be aware of the dangers of such evaluations in order to prevent negative outcome.

i. It is believed that an effective & skilled trainer does not require any formal mid-course evaluation more so if it is a short course of a week or two. Such trainer can perceive, feel and even pick up such feedback through informal channels during tea/coffee and lunch breaks.

ii. The trainer can formalize the process by asking the trainees to describe their feelings at the end of the day. Good feelings are reported from an effective training and vice versa. The trainer, depending on the flexibility can take positive action wherever possible.

iii. The trainer must be confident that in the event of suggestion given by the trainees, he/she should have flexibility, time and resources to address them; otherwise the training will start showing negative effects.

iv. Role of opinion leaders cannot be overlooked in the mid-course review. Few participants may emerge as leaders & tend to influence the opinion of other members.

v. Excessive socialization of trainer & participants may hinder the achievement of the objective. This is further influenced by Halo effect where the trainee's personal likes or dislikes influence one's assessment of the trainer.

vi. Prefer to conduct mid-course review for long term courses & that too after the completion of the modules.

vii. In case of use of rating scales, let participants give reasons why they rate in a particular direction.

viii. Too much evaluation or too many questionnaires can put off the trainees and can become counterproductive for more than one reason. The trainees may stop learning and acquire the role of evaluators or the responses given may be perfunctory.

ix. When trainees are unhappy with few sessions, there are chances of more participants switching off the remaining inputs. Such events need careful handling.

Post Training Evaluation:

Information about the trainees' reaction to training may be obtained during the training immediately after training or sometimes later. End of course reactions are collected using rating scales. Rating scales are forms on which trainees are asked to tick on a number of seven or five point scale.

Specimen:

The session was:
Totally Useless 1 2 3 4 5 Extremely Useful

The information on the forms can be quickly analyzed in form of histograms, charts and results can be feedback to the trainees for group discussion and self analysis. Information on long term reactions can be obtained by questionnaires and/or interviews some time after the end of a course. The inputs can help restructuring the training sessions.

Learning Evaluation:

The purpose of evaluation at this stage is to obtain information on the amount of learning acquired during training programme, irrespective of whether the participants go on to apply the learning on the job. The learning can be divided into Knowledge, Skills and attitudes.

Knowledge Learning

Knowledge Learning can be evaluated by various forms of tests and examinations. The purest form of evaluation of knowledge learning is that used in *Programmed Instruction* where knowledge is evaluated at every stage of the learning process. However, even if programmed learning is not being used, it is possible to construct *Objective Tests* consisting of multiple choice questions.

Academic tests may be constructed where a mere objective test may not be suitable & the knowledge may have a large element of 'Intellectual understanding'.

For open ended training, where training objectives are not formulated in measurable terms, the best way to assess knowledge changes is to ask trainees their knowledge has improved.

Another way to evaluate open ended training is simply to ask the trainees to state "what is the most important or most relevant point they remember from the exercise". This also can be done at the end of each session and can give surprisingly relevant feedback which is useful both to the trainers as an aid to restructure the programme and to the trainees as an aid to memory.

In order to measure the amount of change caused by the training, a test can be conducted at the start of the training programme.

Learning of principles, facts, concepts and skills is easier to measure through standardized test but in other areas of training, the trainer has to devise other techniques of measurement, their exact nature being dependent upon the programme in question.

Training managers are usually a little hesitant of designing tests and questionnaire and tend to restrict outcome to reaction feedback. Training specialists should devote more attention to developing before and after and other measures in order to set up self correcting training systems.

Skill Learning

Skill objectives are always more important that knowledge objectives. Knowledge being a pre-requisite to skill, evaluation of a skill can help identify the learning that has taken place in terms of knowledge. Evaluation instruments must be tailor made to suit the type of skill being evaluated. Since skills are acquired by actual practices, they can be best evaluated by observing and analyzing actual performance of trainees while they are practicing.

The essential requirements are that the skill under training should be observed and analyzed into its behavioural elements. Skills analysis provides techniques for repetitive manual operations and task analysis or non repetitive managerial and social jobs the task must:

1) Be based on crucial elements of the Job;
2) Use only such skills as can be learned during a brief learning period;
3) Be sufficiently complicated to allow a range of observable errors to be made;
4) Be capable of being carried out within a reasonable time.

Skill training requires regular follow up in coordination with the participants.

Attitude Learning

Most training has attitude objectives as well as knowledge and skill objectives. In order to change the attitude in the required direction, the attitude objectives should be clearly defined.

Measuring improvement in attitudes is fraught with difficulties. Attitude exist only in mind, they cannot be directly inferred from people's behaviour. People will reveal their attitude (values, beliefs and opinions) if they

i) Know what they are
ii) Choose to reveal them

A common way of evaluating attitudes and opinions is to hand out a questionnaire at the start and the end of the programme. The questionnaire may be Thurston or a Likert type or it may contain a series of questions with multiple choice answers. The questions must be constructed in light of the attitudinal objectives and interpreted at the face value. Thus an evaluator can choose whether to use standardized tests or generate his own attitude scales.

Specimen:

	Strongly Disagree	Disagree	Neutral	Agree	Strongly Agree
I like to work to be predictable	-2	-1	0	1	2
I like taking risks in things I do at work	-2	-1	0	1	2

The problem with the questionnaires is whether they reflect authentic response of the trainee. Attitude survey would also help in pre- and post training evaluation for areas like managerial behaviour.

Job Behaviour Evaluation

Job Behaviour Evaluation is the crucial half way stage between training and ultimate effects.

Evaluators of Job behaviour have always been worried about the problem of observer bias which can take two forms:
i) The trainee may behave differently because he is being observed.
ii) The observer may be biased.

In case of first, if the trainee is genuinely cooperating in evaluation, he/she will not only provide raw facts about his job behaviour but will discuss with the evaluator the reasons for his behaviour. The second problem of trainers' subjective interpretations remains.

In discussing methods of Job behaviour evaluation, we shall regard the trainee himself as the main source of information, and we shall regard the evaluator as being primarily a catalyst whose aim is to achieve a rapport with the trainee. This would help the trainee to understand his own behaviour and plan to change it. In some other situations evaluations alone is so effective that no other training is necessary, the evaluation itself is training.

Methods of measuring Job Behaviour Evaluation

The methods may be classified into 2 themes.
- *Watching and Asking*
- *Questionnaires/Interview*

Another distinction exists between methods whose aim is to survey the whole of a person's job behaviour and those whose aim is to obtain detailed information about a particular aspect of that behaviour. This is the distinction between *Width* and *Depth*. The 2 dimensions of watching v/s asking and Width v/s depth is shown below.

Exhibit: Methods of Job Behaviour

Width	
Watching	**Asking**
1. Activity Sampling 2. Wirdenious Techniques 3. SISCO 4. Observer Diaries	1. Self Diaries 2. Width Interviews 3. Self Appraisal and appraisal by superior 4. Critical Incident method
Depth	
1. Observation of specific incidents (Unstructured) 2. Open ended depth techniques (Structured)	1. Self reporting of specific incidents 2. Questionnaires on specific behaviour

I. **Width Techniques**

> **Watching**

A. Activity Sampling- evaluator records his observation on the trainee's behaviour at random interval of time.
B. Wirdenious Technique- Developed by Wirdenious to overcome the superficiality of observation in activity sampling. Observer first makes snapshot observation and records what he sees the trainee doing and then goes up to the trainee and asks him what he was in fact doing.
C. SISCO- Developed in London School of Economics. In SISCO, the observer stays with the individual trainee over a period of time and records his behaviour at regular intervals.
D. Observer Diaries- Observer makes record of all the activities carried out by the trainee. The technique is costly and time consuming yet better compared any other method.

> **Asking**

A. Self Diaries- This is an alternative to Observer diaries or activity sampling. This self diary is to be completed by the trainee himself. They are useful in studying managerial behaviour.
B. Width Interviews- They are designed to obtain information about the whole range of trainee's job rather than about the details of one particular aspect. They are most often used as supplement to other evaluation techniques rather than independently by themselves. Width interviews range from structured questionnaires with forced choice answers being required to set questions, to completely informal and open ended questions.
C. Appraisal and self-appraisal- This is better compared to other width techniques. Trainee and supervisors are in better position to appraise due their understanding in greater detail.
D. Critical Incident method- The appraisers are asked to provide descriptions of incidents that are typical of effective or ineffective performance in a Job.

II. Depth Techniques

Depth techniques are mainly of two kinds: Close ended and Open-ended

In close ended techniques, the essential questions are: have the laid objectives of job behaviour achieved? If so, to what extent and I what way? Open ended approach, the basic questions are: has the training led to any changes in job behaviour? If so, describe these changes in detail.

Closed ended Depth Techniques

They must be tailor made to fit the job behaviour objectives of training. In case of repetitive tasks, skills analysis and task analysis provide a complete evaluation of job behaviour as well as learning level.

Observation:

Evaluator observes the trainee while he/she carries out the job, for example, communication skills.

Coaching Approach:

The best person to observe is the trainee's supervisor. This can be regarded as coaching approach. Here the objective is not only to observe and assess the trainee's behaviour but also to help him/her to improve.

Self-Reporting:

Trainees' themselves provide the information about their detailed behaviour. Often this is conducted using interviews and general questionnaires.

Interviews and questionnaires:

Interviews and questionnaires can also be used as close ended depth techniques.

Open ended Depth Techniques:

These are adopted in case of absence of behavioural objectives, which specify precise criteria for evaluation. The evaluator must find out whether the trainee's behaviour has changed in any way as a result of training/ learning acquired and if so, has it been beneficial.

The trainee provides examples of specific incidents in which the reported behaviour changes were demonstrated.

The interview assesses the whole of reaction, learning, Job Behaviour and end results.

Likewise even the trainee's superior could be interviewed to understand about the type of behavioural changes in the trainee.

Job Improvement Plan:

Job improvement plan is an individual action plan and its analysis has to be trainee specific. Each trainee transferred the learning to the job in his work context based on:
i) The areas of his work he plans to improve-Quality, Quantity, Time, Cost
ii) The time frame he envisages for its implementation.
iii) Back home organizational climate –facilitators and inhibitors to be managed for implementing his job improvement plan.

Ultimate Value Evaluation:

The trainee's boss can enable the trainee to translate the improved job-behaviour into perceptible measurable benefits by ensuring post training debriefing discussion with special reference to trainee's job improvement plan. The pressure to catch up with the inevitable in-tray might discourage the trainees to talk of any change. If the trainer does not get involved in such debriefing meetings, it would still be worthwhile to have note of such meeting. Further data can be gathered by use of questionnaires given to trainees & supervisors, direct observations, activity sampling, semi-structured interviews etc.

Follow-Up results:

Based on data gathered, evaluation can be attempted after a gap of 3 to 6 months after the training. This is to seek information regarding application of the learning and job improvement plan. It will enable the trainer to learn why job improvement could not be put into action and in which areas of learning so that it helps him to modify trainings in future.

The valued ends and measures of achievement are generally financial in nature. It is relatively easy to measure the costs incurred on training. The problem is to measure the financial returns on training. According to Jones, there are three possible economic results of training in a firm.

1. To get people to make their full contribution as soon as possible (training time)
2. To continue this contribution in time process as long as possible (retention time of this contribution in the job)
3. To improve on the experienced worker standard (EWS) allowed for in the firm's costing system. i.e. show the profit in performance defined comprehensively as the total contribution to the firm.

Cost benefit analysis has been used for evaluating. Peter Bramley has suggested the following methods:

I. Impact Analysis:

At the pre-training stage, the 'stakeholders' conduct a workshop to arrive at the ultimate outcome of the training intervention. Evaluation a year later, the outcomes is measured. In case of Bramley, the outcomes were:
- Positive movement in their revenue
- Reduction in recruitment of technical staff
- Introduction to new training courses. Demand for training exceeded supply
- Rough estimates showed four percent financial returns.

II. Aspects of organizational effectiveness:
- Achieving targets
- Attracting Resources
- Satisfying interested parties
- Internal processes like transfers, absenteeism, and accident rates

III. Total Quality management:
One criteria of organizational effectiveness is offered by TQM model.

IV. Team effectiveness:
According to this approach, it is the team and not the department of the organization that achieves the targets and is therefore a viable method for evaluating training results.

V. Key result areas:
Evaluating the achievement of key result areas at the individual level would be sufficient indicators to measure training results.

Conclusion:

If one questions the expensiveness of the training evaluation in terms of time, money and resources, the point that it is better than no evaluation at all negates it. To optimize the results, the evaluator must:
1. Possess the knowledge, skills and right attitude about the usage of the methods available to him/her
2. Tap the resources to perform the evaluation
3. Use the data generated appropriately
4. Match the cost of evaluation with the output
5. Prevent excessive use of tests, questionnaires, interviews which may get in the way of learning.
6. Elicit the cooperation of the sponsors of training, the line manager and the trainee in the process.

CHAPTER – 5

Criteria & approaches for Selection of Evaluation Methods

Introduction

We have learnt about the methods available for evaluation at each stage of training. Here we would discuss on how to pick and choose the methods for a given training. The table below indicates the criteria to evaluation.

WHO wants Evaluation	WHY want Evaluation	Approach	Outcome	Look For
Top Management, Sponsors	Total Impact, Returns on Investment	Ultimate Value Client Centered External training	Control	Conclusive and Qualified data
Trainee's Boss, Line Managers Training Utilizers, Trainees	Improved Job Performance, Learning Index	Training Centered	Feedback	Critical Incidents and Boss's Feedback
Training Managers, Trainer, Training Institutions	Reaction Index, Transfer of Training	Training Centered	Intervention	Qualitative, Directive data, Job Improvement Plan

Ultimate Value Approach:

The investment in the training is supposed to ultimately result in some benefit to the organization. Training is essentially a means to end. In a business enterprise management would prefer to measure all its investment in financial terms.

The cost benefit analysis is calculated in 'qualitative terms' and is mostly 'conclusive'. Suppose a company trains their sales force to promote their products in the market, the formulation of evaluation criteria would involve measurement of sales efficiency and probability through financial indicators and may be able to conclude whether profitability has increased or not.

Eventually outcome of evaluation-based training on cost benefit criteria helps in retaining training policy to:

i) Organizational Goals;
ii) Estimating the cost of providing training activity is worth sponsoring at all
iii) Deciding whether a particular training activity is worth sponsoring at all.

Some trainers perceive such controls evaluating criteria as a threat to the training department but actually trainers can use this approach to their advantage by highlighting the contributions of training department.

External training:

Choosing the right criteria for evaluating external training is far more difficult as the ultimate value for the training organization is different from the stakes of the client organization. The client organization sends people for training with the hope that as a result of training, the trainee will bring some improvement in his/her performance and in the organization resulting in some financial returns to them.

Trainee Centered Approach:

If the trainee is the ultimate beneficiary of any training then growth and development of individual is primary, and the cost incurred on training is secondary. Apart from his/her reactions to training, evaluation has to be focused on the criteria of learning and improvement in his

Job performance. It starts with the Job analysis to identify the Job requirements and then train people to fit into that Job.

The feedback could be in form of:
i) Critical incidents, which justify effectiveness of the training.
ii) Before and after measures of levels of knowledge, skills, attitudes and behaviour;
iii) Extent to which objectives set for the programme were met.

Training Centered Approach:

The most convenient & simple is the training centered approach. The trainer has won the half battle if the reactions are positive. The trainer may try to cater the needs of the trainees other than learning in order to ensure positive –reactions and praise for training. Trainer* however would not be contented with mere reactions, & would look for:
i) Signs of transfer of training to the client organization.
ii) Content Analysis of Job improvement Plan showing the degree of transfer facilitated through training;
iii) Encouraging supervisors and line managers to be involved in pre- and post briefing and debriefing.
iv) Ensuring proper selection of participants.

The outcomes may serve as strategic interventions during the course of training. In order to satisfy the ever-growing needs of the buyer's market, the trainer is always looking for qualitative feedback that directs him for further improvement. Ina training centered approach, the trainer tends to use his past experience and sometimes even intuitive impressions to set the reactive evaluation criteria.

CHAPTER – 6

Techniques of Measurement and Its related Problems

Introduction

Measurement is a set of rules for assigning numbers to objects, entities or individuals. A psychological measuring device is a set of rules for assigning numbers to an individual, boss/trainee/trainer that represent a level of some particular psychological trait, attribute or behaviour of the individual. These characteristics may be observable directly on job performance or may be inferred indirectly through changes in responses on job behaviour to a set of stimulus (training).

The assumption below is that there are individual differences in perceptions, beliefs, interest, attitudes and behaviour. Measurement encompasses devising systematic procedures for translating these individual differences into quantitative numeric terms.

Quantitative Approaches of Measuring:

Methods of Data Collection:

Measurement encompasses obtaining information using various data collection techniques as observation, interviews, questionnaire, rating scales, paper and pencil tests, work samples, simulation, job performance, individual and group performance measures, individual and group behaviour measures.

Techniques of Measurement:

1. **Observation:**

Observation is a direct, objective and reliable for m of measurement for understanding human behaviour. Systematic observation is considered as the hallmark strategy for planning and evaluation of training programmes. The function of observation is the conversion of an ongoing complex array of behavioural events into a complete set of data that can influence training needs and decisions.

Recent advances in observational methodology and technology tend to stem from fields of study and practice in which the focus is on interpersonal exchange such as techniques of communication used by workers in an industry, differential behaviour of the workers towards the hierarchical pattern of power in an organization. Observation of trainees before and after the training can provide qualitative and quantitative measurement of behaviour. For this purpose, the specific domains of behaviour should be broken into recordable units for translating informal behavioural observations into formal scientific observations for evaluation.

The important aspect requiring decision making on the part of the observer are:
i) What behaviour to observe and whether the sample behaviour is representative of broad domain of the training programme.
ii) The setting in which the behaviour will be observed.
iii) The length time for observing the behaviour.
iv) Who will observe the behaviour?
v) Coding and analysis of the data.

Types of Observation:

Observation may take many forms. It can range from most natural uncontrolled observations to most exact recordings of training sessions. Observation in natural environments is although less controlled but the efforts and the expenses are huge. Classroom setting have the asset of being more controlled so that behaviour of both participants and trainer can be observed under more standard conditions. The actual observations must be made on the job.

Observation can be participant and non participant. In participant observation, the evaluator becomes member of the employee group and participates in their activities so that he can gain insight into the dynamics of the group. In non participant observation, evaluator remains unobtrusive and observes the trainees' activities from the distance.

Aids in Observation:

Range of tools can be employed like schedules of information, checklists etc. Checklists provide numerical measures of observation. The sessions can be also be recorded & studied later.

Live vs. Recorded Observations:

Research study shows that the presence of an observer alters the behaviour of the subjects. Reactivity to recordings is much less and do not evoke an initial orienting response. In general, video and audio recorded data help to improve accuracy.

Pros and Cons of Observation:

Observation has the following strengths as an assessment tool:
i) Flexible in providing various kinds of data, such as counts of individual behaviours, records of sequences of events etc.
ii) Measures are relatively simple and can be readily obtained.
iii) Observations have a wide range of applicability across different trainee groups, behaviours and organizational settings.

The weaknesses are:

i) Observation is expensive and labour intensive as compared to indirect measures like self-report.
ii) Observations cannot access inner experiences that are unobservable.
iii) Observations give only a limited snapshot of behaviour from which it is difficult to draw generalization.

2. Interview:

The interview is perhaps the most ubiquitous method of obtaining information from people. It is the oldest & perhaps most widely used technique known.

Interview is a scientific tool of data collection in training evaluation. Interview is an effective conversation between persons to achieve consciously selected purpose.

It involves both verbal and non verbal conversation. It is the description of the situation as the evaluator sees from inside out.

Interview is both an art and a science. It provides the evaluator a degree of freedom to exercise one's skills and resourcefulness.

Purposes of Interview:

Interviews are means to an end. They are used to elicit both qualitative as well as quantitative data on complex issues like beliefs, attitudes, feelings and behaviour of the trainees. They can provide a basis for prediction, understanding and action, thereby providing an effective tool for assessment of ultimate value of training.

Types of Interview:

There are many forms of interviews ranging from fact finding to emotional release. Interviews may be classified as structured or unstructured and Directive or non-directive.

- *Structured interviews* are controlled, guided and directive. A detailed pre-planned schedule & a structured format are used. There are predetermined questions asked to every participant in the same manner.
- *Unstructured interviews* are unguided, uncontrolled and non-directive. The questions are not predetermined and the interviewee has the freedom of expressing his/her ideas, thoughts or feelings about the theme in question.
- *Selection Interview-* Used for selection of personnel for certain jobs. This assesses whether the candidate is well equipped with

the skills required for the Job. This can be used as selection for trainees for various training programmes.

- *Focused Interview-* The interview is focused on subjective experiences, attitudes and emotional reactions to particular training situations.
- *Case History Interview-* In case history interview, a complete personal & social history is taken. Focus is on concrete facts, dates and events and trainee's feelings about them. The purpose of the case history is to place the trainees' problems in proper historical developmental context to determine the implications for remedial training.
- *Depth Interview-* Depth interview is intensive. It aims to elicit unconscious feelings like desires, passion, fears related to the personality of the trainee. It assists in the process of self- discovery and to achieve insights. It is used for job behaviour evaluation.
- *The repeated interview-* it attempts to trace the development of a social or psychological process. It is useful in studying attitudes of trainees in the process of formation. Interviews are conducted at regular intervals to know the gradual change in patterns of leadership, communication skills, etc. the briefing and debriefing sessions between trainee and his boss is a case in point.
- *The Crisis Interview-* The interview aims to comfort or advise troubled workers in their critical moments. The aim of such interviews is to meet the problem as they occur and to provide an immediate relief. The purpose is to deflect the potential for a disaster. The advantages of a crisis interview would accrue if a sensitive trainer includes such critical incidents in future training programmes to enhance the capabilities of workers to deal with such crisis. Such interviews require sensitivity and judgment on the part of a trainer.
- *The Research Interview-* These interviews tend to be structured and oriented towards eliciting specific information. The data can be collected from the informants for the purpose of research on training evaluation.
- *The Pre-test and the Post-test interview-*In pre-test –interview, rapport is built to facilitate the testing process. The trainer

communicates the aim and the nature of the test procedures. The goal of pre-test is to check out the characteristics which can affect the test results. The data obtained on pre-test is used to formulate the trainees' baseline evaluation.

- *The post-test interview-* represents an opportunity to checkout hypothesis generated in the course. The post-test interview technique can be used for all stages of evaluation namely reaction, learning, behaviour and ultimate value. The goal is to produce the data, which will enhance the utility of the training results.

Essential element of a good interview is relationship between the trainee and the trainer. Good rapport can be an instrument by which an evaluator achieves the purposes of the interview. When the atmosphere is permissive and harmonious, the interview can yield results.

In addition, attitudes of understanding, acceptance, sincerity and empathy are important techniques of interview. Good communication skills, both verbal and non verbal are of crucial importance to facilitate a good interview. Of extreme importance is the use of appropriate language. Listening is a crucial ingredient of an interview. The use of appropriate questions can facilitate communication in the interview. Open ended questions encourage the trainees to respond in many ways that are more revealing in training evaluation.

Interview Recording:

The facts revealed in an interview are required to be recorded appropriately. A moderate controlled degree of note taking, keeping a tab on phrases used, or recording the interview in an appropriate media could be helpful.

Interviewer Bias:

A major source of problem arises due to preferences and personality of the evaluator. Pre-existing conceptions and beliefs of the trainer contributes to the unreliability of the interview. Selective perception, sensitivity to certain aspects of one's behaviour, projection of trainer's own needs and expectations on to trainees etc can distort the results.

Merits and Demerits of Interviews:

Personal interview yields good and relevant information. It ensures qualitative as well as quantitative measures. The face-to-face contact provides enough stimulation to the participants to probe deeper and complex themes. The interviewer acts as a catalyst. Because of flexibility, the interview is a superior technique for exploration of deeper areas of training evaluation.

The interview has limitations of imposing heavy demand in terms of cost, energy, and time. Training and skills of the evaluator are of importance for obtaining accurate data in the interview. Interviewer's bias can contaminate the interview findings.

3. Questionnaire:

The use of questionnaires in the process of assessment and measurement continues to grow in popularity. Objective Questionnaire has the potential to independently document both the training needs and quantify the efficacy of the training programmes.

A questionnaire is a measurement tool consisting of a set of questions designed to elicit information about the subject. It is a device for securing answers to questions using a form, which the respondent fills. The questionnaire contains a series of questions that may differ in degree of difficulty or depth of probing but logically related to the central problem of training.

Questionnaires are standardized instruments that require standardized responses to similarly formatted descriptive statements, which can generate estimates on a variety of dimensions of training programme.

By using questionnaires one can document the effect of training and establish individual profiles and sets of group profiles. Interpretive handbook can be developed to support training applications. Interest in measuring training effectiveness will make a meaningful contribution to identifying optimal training strategies.

Generally the questionnaire is mailed to the boss/trainees with directions to return it by mail. The appropriateness will depend on:
- type of information required
- Type of respondent
- Accessibility of respondents
- The precision of questions

Questionnaires measure the participants' attitudes about the areas which may be affected by training.

Types of Questionnaires:

Questionnaires can be classified into structured and unstructured. They can be multisource or multidimensional.

A structured questionnaire consists of definite direct and preordained questions regarding various facets of training. Answers to these questions are to be given with high precision without ambiguity. In the unstructured questionnaire, the questions are not structured in advance. The evaluator formulates and asks the questions according to the training situation. The unstructured questionnaire is used mainly for conducting interviews. The chief merit is flexibility. This form of questioning assumes insight, articulateness and revelation of facts by the trainees.

Questions can be based on highly specific items like input evaluation or context evaluation to broad themes of training outcomes. The questionnaire can have close form questions wherein trainee is given little leeway in answering. The answers fall in predetermined categories like 'yes' or 'no'. These are difficult to be constructed but more easily scored. The questionnaires can be open ended where the trainee is given more latitude in answering. The presumed advantage is that it can be used for depth interviews.

Construction of a Questionnaire:

Before formulating a questionnaire, the evaluator should determine what the important questions to be asked are. The construction of a questionnaire encompasses complete knowledge of the topic and advance preparation of the theme. The evaluator has to decide the critical aspects of training evaluation as to whether he wants to assess immediate reaction of the trainees or learning's. Accordingly, the questions should be properly worded, arranged, codified and duly protested and approved by the experts.

A questionnaire must be limited in length and scope. The construct validity and development of empirically based interpretive guidelines are pre-requisite for a questionnaire to achieve status as an established measurement tool.

Merits and Demerits of a Questionnaire:

The Questionnaire is economical in terms of time, effort and cost. It is easy to plan, construct, administer and analyze. It can cover a large universe of training world, which may not be possible with other measurement tools.

On the other side, Questionnaire gives data on a biased sample because it can only be used with selected interested groups. The non-responses in questionnaires are known to be high.

Rating Scales:

Of the psychological measurement methods that depend on human judgments, rating scale procedures exceed them all for popularity and use. They are used in evaluation of individuals, their reactions and their products. The great ease with which they can be administered gives them unusual appeal.

Rating scale represents the single most common measure of trainees' performance. These methods are primarily used for systematizing and structuring the collection of data of training results.

Forms of Rating Scales:

The forms of rating scales in common use in training fall into 5 broad categories: Numerical, Graphic, Cumulated Points, Standard and forced choice technique.

1. **Numerical Scales:**

In a typical numerical scale, a sequence of defined numbers is supplied to the evaluator who assigns to each attribute an appropriate number in line with these definitions or descriptions. One example of such scale in obtaining ratings of a personality of a trainer is given below:

7- Most Pleasant
6- Moderately Pleasant
5- Mildly Pleasant
4- Indifferent
3- Mildly Unpleasant
2- Moderately Unpleasant
1- Most Unpleasant

In some instances, evaluator reports in terms of the descriptive cues about the evaluation of trainees' Job-Behaviour after training. An example would be the following scale for evaluating quality of work.

Excellent
Good
Average
Bad
Poor

2. **Graphic Scales:**

In this method a straight line is drawn and is combined with various cues to aid the rater. The line can be segmented in units or it can be continuous. If segmented, the number of parts can be varied. It can be placed horizontal or vertical.

Rating forms are useful primarily when one or more evaluators must make judgment about the degree and the quality of a particular type of behaviour or Job performance. Some ratings for a series of statements about the behaviour to be measured with a five point frequency scale. These allow the evaluator to indicate his/her judgment of frequency of the behaviour in question. The important point is that the scales must be designed that the responses are quantifiable.

Example:

Rare	Sometimes	A good deal of time	Most of the time	Almost always
1	2	3	4	5

The scale can be easily administered.

3. Standard Scales

The rating scales that come in this category are distinguished by the fact that they present to the evaluator a set of standards with pre-established scale values.

Other rating scale forms that conform more or less to this principle is *Man-to-Man* scale. In this scale a "yardstick" for trainer's capabilities is developed with the traits: initiative, self confidence, force, decisiveness, and tact, ability to inspire interest in people and good communication and influencing skills: The trainers to be appointed for training can be matched with this yardstick.

Rating by Cumulated Points

The unique, common feature of this rating scale is in the method of scoring. The score for an individual trainee is the sum or average of a number of points, weighted or unweighted. E.g. Checklist Method

Forced-Choice Ratings

The forced-choice technique was developed primarily for the purpose of rating personnel. The evaluator is asked to say not how much of a trait the trainee has but to say essentially whether he has more of one trait than another of a pair. One of the traits of the pair is valid for predicting some total quality and the other is not, both appearing about equally favourable to most people, or about equally unfavourable.

Problems in Rating Scales

The use of ratings rests on the assumption that the human observer is a good instrument of quantitative observation, that one is capable of some degree of precision and some degree of objectivity.

Constant Errors

The constant errors in ratings are: the error of leniency, the error of central tendency, and the halo effect.

Error of Leniency: Evaluators tend to rate those whom they know well, or in whom they are ego-involved, higher than they should. This is presumably a constant tendency regardless of trait.

Error of Central Tendency: Evaluators hesitate to give extreme judgments and thus tend to displace individuals in the direction of the mean of the total group.

Halo Effect: One judges the trainees in terms of a general mental attitude toward them. Trainers/bosses rate trainees in the direction of general impression about them.

Logical Error: Judges are likely to give similar ratings for traits that seem logically related in the minds of the evaluators.

Constant Error: The tendency for an evaluator to rate others in the opposite direction from himself in a trait. To illustrate, managers who themselves are high on orderliness tend to rate others low in that trait.

Proximity Error: Adjacent traits on a rating form tend to correlate higher than remote ones.

Minimizing Errors: Various experiences with ratings tend to show that the most effective method for improving ratings is in many ways to train raters carefully.

PART- III
Ready to use Templates

Training Proposal Template 1:

About Training Company:

Objective of Training program:
By end of the course, you will able to:
-
-
-

Who should attend the program/Target audience:
-
-

Core Topics of Training Program:
1.
2.
3.
4.

Participants Size: _____ Minimum; _____ Maximum

Training Venue: _____ Training timings: _____

Cost per person:

About Trainer:
- Name:
- Education:
- Experience:
- Achievements:

Clientele:
1.
2.
3.
4.

Authorised Signatory:

Training Proposal Template 2

Training Title:

Training Description:

Training Objectives:
-
-
-

Parts of Training:

Sr No	Objective	Time	Content Outline	Presentation methods	Handouts/ Materials
1					
2					
3					

No of Participants per batch:

Batch Name	Participant's Strength

Venue Details:

Professional fees:

About the Trainer:

Authorised Signatory:

Training Proposal Template 3

Introduction:	
Objective:	
No. Of Participants:	
Suitable For:	
Classroom Facility:	
Session Timings:	
Content of the workshop:	
Methodology used:	
Professional fee:	
Facilitator's Profile:	

Training Need Identification Template 1

	Name of Employee	
	Department:	
General:		
1.	Are you a new employee or a long-standing employee of the company?	
2.	How long have you been in your **present** job?	
Confirmation of Current Duties		
3.	Do you have a Job Description for your job?	Yes　　　　　　　　　No (Go to Q 6)
4.	Is your job accurately described in the Job Description?	Yes　　　　　　　　　No
5.A	If no, what extra duties do you do that need to be added to your Job Description?	
5.B	What duties are no longer part of your job and can be deleted from your Job Description?	

Job Analysis

6.	Describe the tasks you regularly perform that are critical to carrying out your job effectively.		
7.	Describe the type of equipment you are required to use (for example, keyboard, machinery, tools of trade, etc).		

8.	Do you require a high degree of technical knowledge for your job?	Yes	No
9.	How do you work? Please circle		
Alone Part of a team Other (specify below)			
10.	If you work as part of a team, do you perform the same of different work to members of your team?		
11.	To what extent does your job require you to work closely with other people, such as customers, clients or people in your own organisation? Please circle.		
Very little Moderately A lot			
12.	How much autonomy is there in your job, i.e., to what extent do you decide how to proceed with your work? Please circle.		

| Very little | Moderately | A lot |

| 13. | How much variety is there in your job, i.e., to what extent do you do different things at work, using several skills and talents? Please circle. |

| Very little | Moderately | A lot |

Training Need

14.	**To perform your current job:** What training do you still need (either on-the-job or a formal course) to perform your current job competently (e.g., Excel, bookkeeping, English as a second language, etc)?

15.	**To perform other jobs in the organization:** What other roles in the organization would you be interested in doing if a vacancy became available (e.g., transfer to another section, supervisor position, etc)?

16.	**To perform other jobs in the organization:** What training or experience would be required (e.g., machine operation, negotiation skills, Occupational Health and Safety Awareness, etc)?

Future Development Needs

17.	What are your career aspirations?

18.	What training or development do you need to help make this happen (e.g., external degree study, formal meeting procedures, leadership training, etc)?

Recognition of Prior Learning

19.	What training have you attended within the last three years? (This will help identify if any training sessions have been missed or if any refresher training is required.)

20.	What training or skills have you acquired outside your current job that may be relevant to the wider organization?

Action Plan

	Agreed training and development to be provided over the next 12 months: (Record the details of training courses, on-the-job experiences, buddy systems or mentor arrangements, and include the recommended dates the staff member can expect these to occur.)	
	Training	**Date**
1		
2		
3		
4		
5		
6		
	Signature of Staff Member:	
	Signature of Supervisor:	

Training Need Identification/ Assessment Template 2

Part 1: Personal Data

1. Name (Ms/Mr): _____
2. Current position: _____
3. Number of subordinates (if so): _____
4. Department: _____
5. Tel.: _____ Mobile: _____ E-mail: _____
6. Age: _____ yrs

Part 2: Education

Highest Education: Year of Completion:

Part 3: Work Experience (Present / Past Company)

Designation	Company name	Major KRA

Part 4: Training Program attended

Program Name	Major Topics	Marks Obtained	Year of completion

	Part 4: Training Need	

Major KRA of your current Job	Rate yourself (1<Needs improvement> to 5 <Outstanding>)

Employee's Name and Signature:

Training Need Identification/ Assessment Template 3

A. **Personal/Basic Details:**

Name of the Employee:	
Designation:	
Department:	
Date of Joining:	
Age:	
Date:	

B. **Training(s) Required/Recommended**(To be filled by HR based on the evaluation of attached Questionnaire):

Sr No.	Training recommended	Reasons for Training Requirement
1		
2		
3		
4		
5		

C. Professional Details:

1. Do you satisfied with your current Job profile?
   (a) Narrate the reasons for Satisfaction
   -
   -

   (b) Narrate the reasons for Dissatisfaction
   -
   -

2. What kind of training(s) you want to add up in to your existing profile which will help you in enhancing your performance level?
   -
   -
   -

3. What role & responsibilities would you like to add on?
   -
   -

4. Name of the training(s) recommended by your Department Superior?
   -
   -
   -

5. Are you convinced with the training recommended by your Superior? If yes, please specify.

6. Please specify those areas of performance which had direct/indirect impact due to these training(s).
   -
   -
   -

	Employee	*Training Manager*
Name **Sign**		

Training Need Identification Template 4

Organization's Name:_____

Name of employee:_____ Mobile No:_____

Designation:_____ Joining date:_____

Last Promotion date:_____ Designation:_____

1. Write Down Your Major KRA which were mentioned in your Job Profile:
   -
   -
   -

2. Extra work you are doing which is not mentioned in your Job Profile:
   -
   -

3. Describe the tasks you regularly perform that are critical to carrying out your job effectively.

   ....
   ....

4. Describe the type of equipment/instruments you use as a part of your job (for example, Computer, I-Pod, Calculator, Vernier Callipers, Slide rule etc).

   ....
   ....

5. Does your job require a high degree of technical knowledge?   Yes   No

   ....

6. If you work as part of a team, do you perform the same of different work to members of your team? Explain.

7. Do you need to interact with Clients/Customers directly? Please circle.

   Rare   Usual   A lot

8. **To perform your current job:** What training do you still need to perform your current job competently (e.g., Presentation skills, Communication skills, Computer skills)?

9. What other roles in the organisation would you be interested in doing if a vacancy became available?

10. What additional training or experience would be required?

11. How do you see your career with this firm?

12. What training or development do you need to help make this happen?

13. What training have you attended within the last three years?

14. What training or skills have you acquired outside your current job that may be relevant to the organisation?

....

....

Agreed training and development to be provided over the next 12 months:

Training   **Date**

....

....

Signature of Employee   :   ....   **Date:**   ....
Signature of Supervisor   :   ....   **Date:**   ....

Training Need Identification Template 5

Development Plan for functional contribution
- Identify the areas of functional development that directly affect the completion of KRAs.
- The area of development should be linked either to an incomplete objective of the last year or completion of an objective for the coming year

<u>Example</u>

Areas of development	End Objective	Criticality	Responsibility	Time Frame
Supply Chain Management	Set in place the vendor management process	1	Training	3 months

Areas of development	End Objective	Criticality	Responsibility	Time Frame

Development Plan for Personal Effectiveness (P)

Parameter	Observed Behaviour	Action Plan	Criticality	Responsibility	Time Frame

CRITICALITY:

1. High Criticality, required at the earliest for performing on the job.
2. Medium Criticality would help in better performance, not immediate.
3. Nice to know.

Training Need Identification Template 6

Company Name/Letter Head

EMPLOYEE NAME:			POSITION:		TNA DONE BY:	
Major tasks of position	Training/skills development required?		If yes, identify what training needs exist	How will this be achieved? (e.g. on the job, external training)	When?	Who to organise? Training provider?
	Y	N				
	☐	☐				
	☐	☐				
	☐	☐				
	☐	☐				
	☐	☐				

What do we want to achieve in the period ahead?

Where do you/we see your career progressing in the next two years?

How are we going to make this happen?

What will you need from the company to help you to reach your career goals?

Employees Name & Signature

Training Need Identification Template 7

Induction: Staff feedback (1 month)　　　Date: //20_____
Name of Employee: _____
Designation: _____
Section/Unit: _____

1. Were you personally introduced to your new colleagues, managers and other appropriate people during your first few days in post?
   Yes_____ No_____
   Any additional comments:
   -
   -

2. Has your Induction helped you understand your job, responsibilities, work standards?
   Yes_____ No _____
   Any additional comments:
   -
   -

3. Have appropriate policies and procedures, important to your job (health and safety, regulations, work processes), been shown to you and explained to you?
   Yes_____ No _____
   Any additional comments:
   -
   -

4. Have the materials/sections in the Induction Pack been of use to you?
   Yes_____ No _____
   Any additional comments:
   -
   -

5. Have you discussed/completed an Induction Training and Development Plan?
Yes_____ No _____
Any additional comments:
-
-

6. If there was one aspect of your Induction that could be improved what would it be, and how might we improve it?
Aspect:
Suggestions for improvement:

Employee's Name and Signature:

Training Registration Form Template 1

Participant's details

Last Name: [   ]   **First Name:** [   ]

Tel. No. [   ]   **Mobile No.** [   ]

Date of Birth: [   ]   **Email ID** [   ]

Address: [   ]
Postcode: [   ]

Email Address: [   ]

Employment History

Please tell us about your Current job.

Joining Date: [   ]

Name of Employer: [   ]

Current Position: [   ]

Education & Training

Qualifications obtained from Schools, Colleges, Training Providers or previous employers.

Qualifications and/or Training Courses	Dates (from & to)	Grades Obtained
Continue on back of this sheet if necessary		

I hereby certify that all the information given by me on this form is correct to the best of my knowledge

Signed: **Date:**

Training Registration Form Template 2

Training Registration Form	
Registration for:	Training Program Name:
Location/City:	
Program Dates:	
Full Name: (to be in the certificate – limit to max 16 characters)	
Nomination Type (Company Sponsored /Individual):	
Gender:	
Age:	
Nationality:	
Designation:	
Organization:	
Industry sector: (e.g., IT, BPO, Banking, Manufacturing etc.,):	
Functional /Technical expertise (e.g., Java, Quality, HR, Sales etc.,):	
Academic qualifications:	
Industry experience (in yrs):	
Mobile:	

E-mail/Chat id (Personal):	
Will you carry a laptop (Y/N)?	
Previous exposure to the Training Program (if any): (Y/N - details):	
Key Expectations (Why enrolling for this program?):	

Training Registration Form Template 3:

Name of Course: _____

Course Location: _____

Course Date(s): _____ Quoted Course Fee: _____

Registrant(s):

Name	Designation	Email	Mobile

Organisation: _____

I have read, understood and agreed to LEAP Australia's Terms and Conditions, related to training courses, as outlined in the accompanying document.

Signature: _____ Date: _____

Course Fees		No of Registrants		Total payable amount
	*		=	

Payment Options (please choose one):

Cheque	Direct Deposit	Demand Draft	Net Banking

*(**Please Note:** Payment is required at least 7 days prior to the scheduled commencement of the training course.)*

Please email this completed form to: XYZ@ABC.com

Training company: _____
Contact Person's Name: _____ M: _____
Training Company's Address:
_____
_____
_____

Training Design Template 1

Workshop Name: _____   Date: _____
Topic/Subject: _____   Venue: _____

Objective: _____

Session unit	Activity/ Description	Duration/ time slots	Training aids/tools	Trainer/ faculty
1	Describe what will be done in this unit of the session. Include activity such as role play, method used, topic covered etc.	Length/ Duration of time planned for this activity	List out Whatever materials that may be required for this activity- a film, flip charts, handouts, game material, etc.	The role of a trainer/ faculty. the role of the instructor – the participants, guests, etc.
2				
Totals	Total time estimated	Hrs/mins	Total cost estimate: Rs.	

Training Design Template 2

Training No:		Venue:		Date:	
Time	Learning Objective*	Content of Training	Learning Method	Facilitator	Aids Required
(00:00 to 01:30)	At the end of the program Participants will able to	Major Topics you are going to cover	Reference books, Activities, Articles etc…	Name	Audio-Visual, Flip charts, White boards etc.

Training Design Template 3

Topic: _____

Objective: _____
_____
_____
_____

Duration: _____ Number of participants: _____

Check list of Materials required:

Training- Initiating the session
1. Icebreakers/activity _____ minutes

_____
_____

2. Introduce the Topic: _____ minutes

(Motivate participants, show them why the topic is important, and share objectives and agenda.)

Training- The body _____ minutes
(Explain the topic in detail, demonstrate and discuss the concept, practice and apply the topic.)

_____
_____

Note: You may like to consider breaking up content into distinct parts, organizing the sequence and ensure delivery of each smaller unit/sub part.

Training- Closure

- Summarize the Topic: _____ minutes

(Reconnect with the objectives, check for understanding, and discuss questions.)

_____
_____

- Plan Next Steps: _____ minutes

(Be specific about application to immediate practice.)_____
_____
_____

- Closing Comments: _____ minutes

(Acknowledge, motivate, inspire)_____
_____

Training Design Template 4

Training Title:				
Training Objectives:				
Training Type: Annual or Specific			No of Participants:	
Training Venue: In-house/Outbound			Training Language:	
Training Aids:				
1.	Case Study	5.	Lecture	
2.	Role Play	6.	Audio Visual	
3.	Group Discussion	7.	Presentation	
4.	Demonstration and Practice	8.	Handouts, Printed Materials	
Detailed Agenda:				
Sr No	Timeline	Topics	Training Aids	Facilitator
1	09:00 to 09:45	Ice breaking	Group Discussion	Mr./Ms.
2				
3				
4				
5				
Total time				

Training Calendar Template 1

2015	1	2	3	4	5	6	7	8	9	10	11	12	13	14	15	16	17	18	19	20	21	22	23	24	25	26	27	28	29	30	31
Jan		Induction																													
Feb							Fire Safety																								
March																															
Apr									Technical Training																						
May														Soft Skills																	
Jun																															
Jul																															
Aug																															
Sep														Technical Training																	
Oct			Outbound																												
Nov																															
Dec																															

Training Calender2015

Training Calendar Template 2

Sr No	Date	Timings	Training Name	Target Participants	Expected Strength	Trainer Name	Venue
1	03rd Jan to 7th Jan	09am to 11am	Fire safety	Zone 1	35	Mr. XYZ	E Block, Training Hall
2							

Training Calendar Template 3

Training Name	Venue	Date	Jan	Feb	Mar	Apr	May	Jun	Jul	Aug	Sep	Oct	Nov	Dec
Operational Training														
1	■								■					
2			■				■							
3					■					■				
Soft Skill														
1		■												
2				■										
3					■									
Organizational Training														
1									■					
2										■				■
3							■				■			
Computer Skills														
1	■						■					■		

Training Calendar Template 4

Month	Date	Location	Venue	Participants' strength
January			Training Name 1	
		Unit 1		
		Unit 2		
		Unit 3		
		SEZ		
			Training Name 2	
		Unit 1		
		Unit 3		
		Unit 4		
		Unit 6		
		SEZ		
February			Training Name 1	
		Unit 1		
		Unit 6		
			Training Name 2	
		Unit 4		
		Unit 5		

Training Evaluation Template 1

(Individual session evaluation sheet)

Session No. and Title _____

Session leader: _____

Please evaluate the session as it appeared to you in relation to the nine points listed below. Place an X on the scale over the point between the two evaluations so that it indicates where your opinion lies. + indicates the optimum point on the scale.

1. Objective explained:
Poorly   [   ] [   ] [   ] [   ] [+]   Clearly
2. Objective achieved:
No   [   ] [   ] [   ] [+]   Fully
3. Selection of Method of instruction:
Poor   [   ] [   ] [   ] [   ] [+]   Fully appropriate
4. Content:
Over simplified   [   ] [   ] [+] [   ] [   ]   Too sophisticated
5. Participants active involvement:
Too little   [   ] [   ] [+] [   ] [   ]   Too much

6. Leadership provided by Trainer:

   Weak

		+		

   Overdone

7. Handouts and visual aids-quality:

   Poor

		+		

   Excessive

8. Handouts and visual aids-quantity:

   Too few

		+		

   Too many

9. Time allotted:

   Too little

		+		

   Too much

Training Evaluation Template 2

Name of Programme: _____ Date: _____

1. How would you rate the overall programme as an educational experience?									
Excellent		Very Good		Good		Fair		Needs improvements	
2. To what extent will it help you do a better job?									
To a large extent			To some extent				Little		
3. What were the major benefits you received?									
	Helped confirm/clarity some of my ideas								
	Presented new ideas and approaches								
	Acquainted me with problems and solutions from other co's								
	Gave me the stimulus to look objectively at myself & my job								
	Any other benefits								
4. What did you think about the course duration?									
Too Little			About right			Too Much			
5. How were the administrative arrangements?									
Excellent		V Good		Good		Fair		Needs improvement	
6. Were all important subjects covered?									
	Yes					No			
			If Not, give details:							
7. Any other comments/suggestions:									
Name:									Date:
Signature:									

Training Evaluation Template 3

Session wise evaluation sheet			
Name of course:			
Date:			
Sr.No.	Subject	How far did the topic contribute to your learning?		
		Large extent	Some extent	Very little
1				
2				
3				
4				
5				
6				
7				
8				
9				
10				
11				
12				
13				

Any specific suggestions regarding presentation _____
_____
_____

Name /Signature _____

Date: _____

Training Evaluation Template 4

1. On the whole, do you think that the programme content was							
Very Good		Good		Above Average		Below Average		Poor	
2. Do you think there are subjects that should be eliminated?							
Yes				No			
3. Do you think that any other additional subjects should have been covered in the programme?							
Yes				No			
4. Do you think that the length of the programme was							
Too long		Too short				Just right	
5. Was the amount of time appropriate to each subject adequate?							
Yes				No			

6. What is your evaluation of each of the following sessions of the programme? What are your suggestions?

Topic	Faculty	Session evaluation				Mode of communication			
		How far did the topic contribute to your learning							
		Large extent	Some extent	Very little	Not at all	Good	Above average	Below average	poor

7. How do you find?

	Too much	Adequate	Not enough
Reading material			
Overall schedule			

8. What were the major benefits you received

	Helped confirm/clarity some of my ideas
	Presented new ideas and approaches
	Gave me the stimulus to look objectively at myself and my job
	Any other benefits

9. Did you find the audio visual aids useful?

Yes	No

10. Were the exercises in your opinion relevant

Yes	No

11. Would you recommend the programme to others in your organization?

Yes	No

Please state reason:
1.
2.
3.

12. I intend to use the following things which I have learnt during the programme:

1	
2	
3	
4	
5	
6	
7	
8	
9	
10	

Training Evaluation Template 5

Name:		Employee code:			
Department:		Date:			
Particulars	V Good	Good	Average	Okay	Poor
Overall Training Program					
Teaching aids used					
Learning Objective					
Venue					
Training outline					
Participation from other team member					
Facility					
Quality of material distributed					
Trainer's performance					

Positives:
-
-
-
-

Areas of improvements:
-
-
-

Signature:

Training Evaluation Template 6

Please indicate your feedback below.

	Strongly Agree	Agree	Disagree	Strongly Disagree
1. The training met my expectations.	O	O	O	O
2. I will be able to apply the knowledge, what I learned.	O	O	O	O
3. The training objectives for each topic were followed.	O	O	O	O
4. The content was organized.	O	O	O	O
5. The materials distributed were useful.	O	O	O	O
6. The trainer was knowledgeable.	O	O	O	O
7. The quality of instruction was good.	O	O	O	O
8. The trainer met the training objectives.	O	O	O	O
9. Class participation and interaction were encouraged.	O	O	O	O
10. Adequate time was provided for questions and discussion.	O	O	O	O

11. How do you rate the training overall?

Excellent	Good	Poor	Very poor
O	O	O	O

Areas of improvement:

_____

_____

Any other suggestions:
_____
_____

Training Evaluation Template 7

Training Name:
Trainer's name:
Training Date:

Name of the Employee:
Department:

Particulars	Not Applicable	Strongly Disagree	Disagree	Agree	Strongly Agree
1. Overall Training	N/A	1	2	3	4
2. Training content.	N/A	1	2	3	4
3. Practical learning	N/A	1	2	3	4
4. Training design	N/A	1	2	3	4
5. Training Methodology	N/A	1	2	3	4
6. Ambience	N/A	1	2	3	4
7. Knowledge of Trainer	N/A	1	2	3	4
8. Overall performance of trainer	N/A	1	2	3	4
9. Trainer's response to your queries	N/A	1	2	3	4

10. Presentation skills of trainer	N/A	1	2	3	4
11. Participation of other team members	N/A	1	2	3	4
12. Usefulness of the training Program for work	N/A	1	2	3	4
13. Overall learning	N/A	1	2	3	4
Signature of Employee:					

Training Certificate Template 1

Company Logo & Name

Certificate No:

This is to Certify that Mr. /Ms. _____ *has participated for the (Training Program Name) from* ___ *to* ___ *(duration) at* ___ *(Venue).*

Trainer's name & Sign _____

Training Manager's name & Sign
_____

(Training Company Name & Logo)
(Website, Registration/Accreditation)

Training Certificate Template 2

 Certificate

This is to certify that Mr. XYZ has completed the Safety Training Course.
And is Awarded this certificate by
ABC company Ltd.
Date:

Authorised Signature:

Training Certificate Template 3

Organization's Name & Logo

Certificate
Of Training
Participant's Name

Has successfully undergone for the training on
(Training Program name)

Certificate Expiry date: //

Authorised Signature

Training Certificate Template 4

NOTES/REFERENCES

Part 1

Chapter 1

1. Cummings, Thomas & Worley Christopher; *"Organization Development Change"*, Thomson Southwestern Publishing, Seventh Edition, Chapter 1, PP- 1, 2, 3, 4, 5, 9, 11.
2. Cummings, Thomas & Worley Christopher; *"Organization Development Change"*, Thomson Southwestern Publishing, Seventh Edition, Chapter 3, PP- 47.
3. Cummings, Thomas & Worley Christopher; *"Organization Development Change"*, Thomson Southwestern Publications, Seventh Edition, Chapter 23, PP- 614.
4. W. Burke, *Organizational Development: Principles and practices* (Boston: Little, Brown 1982)
5. W. French, *"Organization Development: Objectives, Assumptions, and Strategies,"* California Management review
6. M. Beer, *"Organizational Change and Development; A systems View"*,
(Santa Monica, Calif: Goodyear Publishing, 1980)

Chapter 2

1. Vaughn. Robert H.; *"The Professional Trainer"*, Berrett Koehler Publications, Second Revised Edition, Preface Pp-ix, Foreword pp- xi, Ch1 pp- 1,2,3,4,5.
2. Leigh. David; *"The Group Trainer's Handbook"*, Kogan Page Publications, Third revised Edition, Chapter 1.
3. Koehnert, Gary; *"Basic Training for Trainers"*, Tata Mcgraw Hill Publications, Third Edition, Chapter 1 pp- 1,2,3,4,5,6,7,8,9.
4. O'Connor, Bronner, Delaney; *"Training For organizations"* Thomson Publications, Chapter 5 pp136.
5. Bloom, *"Taxonomy of Educational Objectives, Handbook 2: Affective Domain"* Addison-Wesley
6. Goldstein, Irwin L. & Associates. *"Training and Development in Organizations"*, San Francisco: Jossey-Bass, 1989, pp
7. Web Resources: Articles from
   - www.trainingmag.com
   - T+D Magazine (Published Monthly by ASTD) www.astd.org
   - www.trainingdirectorsforum.com
   - www.masie.com
8. http://www.chairacademy.com/journals/20-2/files/page/9.swf

Chapter 3

1. O'Connor, Bronner, Delaney; *"Training For organizations"* Thomson Publications, Chapter 1, pp-8.

Chapter 4

1. Koehnert, Gary; *"Basic Training for Trainers"*, Tata McGraw Hill Publications, Third Edition, Chapter 2.
2. O'Connor, Bridget, Bronner Michael; Delaney, Chet; *"Training For organizations"* Thomson Publications, Chapter 2
3. Vaughn. Robert H.; *"The Professional Trainer"*, Berrett Koehler Publications, Second Revised Edition, Chapter 3

4. Gupta. Kavita. *"A Practical Guide to Needs Assessment"*, San Francisco: Jossey-Bass, 1998, 224 pp
5. Rothwell. William. J., *"Beyond Training & Development"*, Jaico Publications, Chapter 4.
6. P L Rao, "Enriching Human Capital through Training and Development", Excel Book Publication, Chapter 6, pp 99,100.
7. Web Resources: Articles from
   - www.ispi.org

Chapter 5

1. Koehnert, Gary; *"Basic Training for Trainers"*, Tata McGraw Hill Publications, Third Edition, Chapter 6.
2. Koehnert, Gary; *"Basic Training for Trainers"*, Tata McGraw Hill Publications, Third Edition, Chapter 8.
3. O'Connor, Bridget, Bronner Michael; Delaney, Chet; *"Training For organizations"* Thomson Publications, Chapter 6.
4. Singh, P.N.; *"Training for Management Development"*, Suchandra Publications, Fourth Edition, Chapter 4.
5. Hart. Lois, *"Faultless Facilitation"*, Viva Books Publishing Limited, Chapter 5 PP 68.

Chapter 6

1. Singh, P.N.; *"Training for Management Development"*, Suchandra Publications, Fourth Edition, Chapter 8.
2. Vaughn. Robert H.; *"The Professional Trainer"*, Berrett Koehler Publications, Second Revised Edition, Chapter 6
3. Davies. Eddie, *"The Training Manager's A Handbook"*, Crest Publishing House. Chapter 15.

Part 2

1. Bowen, D.D., Lewicki, R.J., Hall, F.S. and Hall, D.T. Experiences in Management and Organisational Behavior. John Wiley & Sons, Inc. USA, 1997.

2. Fernald, L.D. and Fernald, P.S. Introduction to Psychology. AITBS Publishers & Distributors, New Delhi, 1999.
3. Goode, W.J. and Hatt, P.K. Methods in Social Research. McGraw-Hill Book Company, Japan, 1983.
4. Guilford, J.P. Psychometric Methods. Tata McGraw-Hill Publishing Co. Ltd., New Delhi, 1984.
5. Hockenbury, D.H arid Hockenbury, S.E. Psychology. Worth Publishers, 33, Irving Place, New York, 1997.
6. Mehrens, A.W. and Lehmann, J.I. Measurement and Evaluation in Education and Psychology. CBS College Publishing, Holt, Rinehart and Winston, The Dryden Press, Saunders College Publishing, 1984.
7. Murphy, K.R. and Davidshofer, C.O. Psychological Testing. Principles and Applications.
8. Prentice Hall, Upper Saddle River, New Jersey, 1998.
9. Raj, H. Theory and Practice in Social Research. Surjeet Publications, New Delhi, 1988. Sdorow, L.M. Psychology. International Edition. McGraw-Hill Companies, Inc. USA, 1998.
10. Tosi, Hi., Rizzo, J.R. and Carrol, S.J. Organisational Behaviour. A Comprehensive Manual, Beacon Books, New Delhi, 1998.
11. A.C. Hamblin: "Evaluation of Training", Industrial Training International, Nov. 1970, pp. 33-36.
12. Donald Kirkpatrick: Evaluation of Training. In Ed. Robert L. Craig Training and Development Handbook, McGraw Hill Book Company, New York. 1976, pp. 18-20.
13. Peter Warr: "Evaluating Management Training." Journal of Institute of Personnel Management, Business Publications Limited, London, Feb. 1969.
14. B.R.Virmani and PremilaVerma: "Evaluating Management Training and Development." Vision Books, New Delhi, 1985.
15. Bramley Peter: Evaluating Training. Universities Press (India) Limited. 1997.
16. Reay David: Evaluating Training, Kogan Page Ltd., London, 1995, pp. 71.

17. P L Rao, "Enriching Human Capital through Training and Development", Excel Book Publication, Chapter 7, pp 169, 170, 171, 172, 173.

Part 3

www.tidyform.com
http://y4y.ed.gov.
O'Conner, Bronner, Delaney- 2003
www.pandadoc.com

Suggested Further Reference:

Cummings, Thomas & Worley Christopher; "Organization Development Change", Thomson Southwestern Publishing, Seventh Edition

Vaughn, Robert H.; "The Professional Trainer", Berrett Koehler Publications

Leigh. David; "The Group Trainer's Handbook", Kogan Page Publications, Third revised Edition

Koehnert, Gary; "Basic Training for Trainers", Tata Mcgraw Hill Publications

O'Connor, Bridget, Bronner Michael; Delaney, Chet; "Training for organizations" Thomson Publications

Singh, P.N.; "Training for Management Development", Suchandra Publications, Fourth Edition

Burke, W; "Organizational Development: Principles and practices," Boston: Little, Brown 1982

French, Wendell; "Organization Development: Objectives, Assumptions, and Strategies," California Management review

Beer, Michael; "Organizational Change and Development; A systems View",

Santa Monica, Calif: Goodyear Publishing, 1980

French, Wendell & Bell, Cecil; "Organizational Development", Sixth Edition, Pearson Education.

Beckhard, Richard; "Organizational Development: Strategies & Models", Addison-Wesley Publishing.

P L Rao; "Enriching Human Capital Through Training and Development", Published by Anurag Jain for Excel Books

Porass and Robertson; "Organizational Development: Theory, Practice & Research,"

Clarke, M.C; & R.S. Cafferella; "An Update on Adult Learning Theory," New Directions for Adult & Continuing Education, Monograph No. 84, San Francisco: Jossey-Bass, Winter 1999, 106 pp.

Blanchard, P.N. & Thacker, and J.W; "Effective Training: Systems, Strategies and Practices, Upper Saddle River, New Jersey: Prentice Hall, 1999.

Bloom, "Taxonomy of Educational Objectives, Handbook 2: Affective Domain" Addison-Wesley

Goldstein, Irwin L. & Associates; "Training and Development in Organizations", San Francisco: Jossey-Bass, 1989,

Gupta. Kavita. "A Practical Guide to Needs Assessment", San Francisco: Jossey-Bass, 1998,

Rothwell. William. J.; "Beyond Training & Development", Jaico Publications,

Craig, Robert; "A Handbook of Training & Development".

Rao, T.V & Pareek Udai; "Developing Motivation through experiencing"

Pareek, Udai& Lynton, Rolf. P.; "Training for Organizational Transformation, part 1 & 2".

Beich, Elaine; "Training for Dummies".

Hart. Lois; "Faultless Facilitation", Viva Books Publishing Limited, Chapter 5 PP 68.

Davies. Eddie; "The Training Manager's A Handbook", Crest Publishing House. Chapter 15.

Kemp, J.E; "Designing Instructional Systems," Palo Alto, CA: Fearon, 1964, 166 PP.

Van Adelsberg, David and Edward. A. Trolley; "Running Training like a Business: Delivering Unmistakable Value," San Francisco: Berrett-Koehler, 1999, 218 PP

Easterby Smith, M., Evaluating Management Training and Education, Second Edition, Gomer, 1994.

EFQM Total Quality Management, The European Model for Self-Appraisal. The Europeon Foundation for Quality Management, Brussel Belgium. 1995.

Henerson M.E., Morris, L.I. and Fitzgibbon, C.T. How to measure attitudes, Beverley Hills, Sage Publications, 1978.

International Labour Organization: An introductory course in Teaching and Training Methods for Management Development Sterling Publishers, Pvt Ltd., 1983

Leslie Rae: How to Measure Training Effectiveness, Gower Publishing Limited, England.

Robert L. Craig (Ed). Training and Development Handbook. McGraw Hill Book Company, New York, 1976.

Walters M. Employee Attitude and Opinion Surveys. London, IPD. 1966.

Web Resources:

www.businessperform.com
www.teacher.org
www.trainingmag.com
www.astd.org
www.trainingdirectorsforum.com
www.masie.com
www.ispi.org
www.hronline.com
www.workforceonline.com

www.ingramcontent.com/pod-product-compliance
Lightning Source LLC
Chambersburg PA
CBHW032001170526
45157CB00002B/488